Contents

Y0-BEO-864

© HMH Supplemental Publishers Inc. All rights reserved.

Summarizing Strategies Grade 6, SV 9781419099

Introduction

Throughout their school career, students are asked to read a variety of materials, from long stories and challenging poems to brief, informative articles and in-depth reports. Regardless of the genre and length of what they read, students must be able to summarize new information. A *summary* is a brief statement that tells the important points of a work of fiction or the main ideas of a work of nonfiction.

Summarizing is a fundamental reading and study skill. Young readers who master this skill have a powerful tool that helps them
- check their comprehension of what they have read.
- create their own materials for later study and review.
- organize information in various patterns.
- paraphrase new information in words that are meaningful to them.
- perform better on standardized test items that require summary.

Not only does summarizing help students gauge their reading comprehension, it reveals the underlying organizational patterns of writing. Students can then use these patterns as they write their own fiction and nonfiction pieces.

In early grades, summarizing is often taught in conjunction with identifying main idea and important details. As students progress, they learn to extract important information from a greater variety of genres and to generalize, draw conclusions, and make inferences as part of summarizing.

This series, *Summarizing Strategies,* is comprised of five books (Grades 2–6) and suggests a variety of techniques to encourage summarizing skill development. Each book targets 21 different strategies and employs a diverse collection of graphic organizers to assist students in visualizing how summaries are formed. Graphic organizers are critical components that serve as scaffolding necessary for students to structure their summaries and make connections between the targeted strategy and summarizing.

The strategies are logically sequenced from most basic to most difficult. Students begin by looking for the main idea and supporting details. As they progress through the book, students will encounter increasingly complex skills that require them to use higher-order thinking skills.

arcourtschoolsupply.com
Supplemental Publishers Inc. All rights reserved.

Features

Each of the 21 strategies follows a four-page sequence. The first page contains a completed model graphic organizer and summary based on the targeted strategy.

Students first learn about the strategy they will practice.

Sample reading selection is geared toward targeted summarizing strategy.

A completed model is provided for students to follow.

The second and third pages of each section provide reading passages adapted for each strategy. After reading each story, students continue to the worksheet page to complete the graphic organizer and write a summary based on what they have read in the story.

Students may practice reading independently, in small groups, or with the whole class.

Simple, clean designs and illustrations allow for clear photocopies and easy-to-read transparencies.

© HMH Supplemental Publishers Inc. All rights reserved.

Summarizing Strategies Grade 6, SV 9781419099

The fourth page in each section is a worksheet featuring a specific graphic organizer created for each strategy. These worksheets are designed for use with the provided texts as well as any other readings the teacher may choose, allowing for extra practice as needed. Worksheet pages are easily found by looking for the Teacher's Toolbox icon:

Students practice the summarizing strategies by completing the worksheets with graphic organizers.

A large graphic organizer is provided so that students can assemble information from the text.

Students then apply the strategy to write a brief summary.

When compiled, these 21 template pages form a Teacher's Toolbox of Graphic Organizers. This feature has been designed to allow flexibility and adaptation for a wide range of texts and student skill levels.

Teacher's Toolbox of Graphic Organizers

Center on the Main Idea	8	Implied Idea	52
Supporting Pillars	12	Sequence Peacock	56
Spoke and Wheel	16	Fact Fingers	60
Theme Map	20	Prediction Chart	64
Compare-Contrast Chart	24	Cause and Effect Meltdown	68
Plot Sequence Chart	28	Cause with Multiple	
Q Matrix	32	Effects Diagram	72
Bright Idea	36	Author's Purpose Table	76
Plot Pie Chart	40	Conclusion Train	80
Character Motivation Table	44	Following Footprints	84
Character Profile	48	Generalization Pyramid	88

Summarizing Strategies uses a variety of techniques to improve students' abilities to summarize. With continued practice in summarizing, students should improve their reading comprehension skills and standardized test scores.

upplemental Publishers Inc. All rights reserved.

Summarizing Strategies Grade 6, SV 9781419099908

Main Idea

Presentation and Model

Strategy: Finding and stating the main idea of what you read

When you state the main idea of something you have read, you are writing a one-sentence summary. The main idea of a reading selection is the most important idea in it. To find this important idea, follow these steps:

- **Read:** Read the paragraphs carefully.
- **Ask:** What topic are the paragraphs about?
- **Decide:** What do all the sentences say about the topic?

Read the story below.

Leah and her dad hiked in the woods on Saturday. The weather was cool, and some clouds were in the sky. "Dad," asked Leah, "do you think it will rain on us?"

"Don't worry. We'll be fine," said her father.

As they walked they spotted many birds in the trees. They waited by a raccoon's den, still and quiet, until the raccoon peeked out. Then they picnicked by the river. Leah looked at the clouds. They were darker now. "Dad," she said nervously, "I think it's going to rain."

"Don't worry! We'll be fine," said her father.

As they hiked back, a light rain began to fall. Leah's father smiled and pulled two rain ponchos from his pack. He pulled one on and helped Leah put on hers. "See?" he said. "Rain or no rain, a hike is fun."

Complete the Center on the Main Idea diagram based on what you've read.

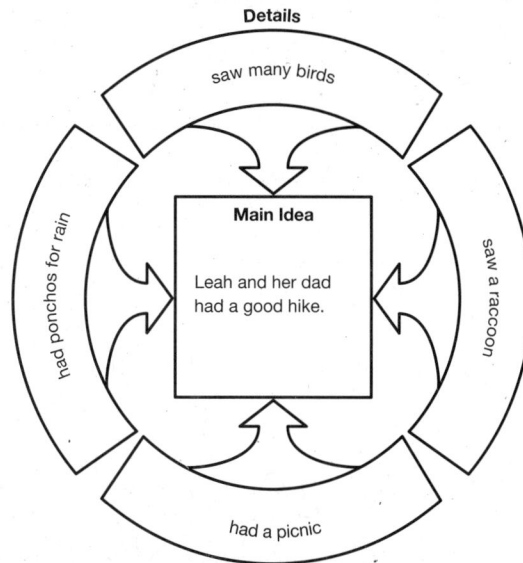

Details

saw many birds

had ponchos for rain

Main Idea

Leah and her dad had a good hike.

saw a raccoon

had a picnic

Summary: Use the information in the Center on the Main Idea diagram to write a summary of the story.

Leah and her dad had a fun hike, even when it began to rain.

© HMH Supplemental Publishers Inc. All rights reserved.

Summarizing Strategies Grade 6, SV 9781419099908

Main Idea

Read the story below.

Game Night

Becca stepped back to look at the table. She was pleased. Everything was set up perfectly for her game night. Her favorite board game was laid out, and she had set out popcorn and lemonade for refreshments. A knock at the door signaled her that her guests had arrived.

Jasmine, Chad, and Hal tossed their coats on the couch and sat down at the table with the games they brought.

"I brought a bingo game," Hal said.

"That sounds like fun," Becca replied.

"I have a game where one person draws pictures and everyone tries to guess what the picture is," said Chad.

Jasmine pulled out some cards and announced, "I decided to bring Old Maid."

"Since Becca has her game set up, let's play it first. Then we'll take turns choosing other games to play," Hal offered. Everyone thought it was a perfect idea for a fun evening.

"Let's get started," Becca said. "This is going to be fun."

Complete the Main Idea Worksheet for this story.

Main Idea

Read the story below.

Amanda's Arm

"There! That will keep the bone safe as it heals," Dr. Bryce had told Amanda before she left his office.

Amanda wasn't comforted by the doctor's words. She didn't care if the bone was safe. All she could think about were all the things she couldn't do with a cast on her arm.

"If only I were right-handed!" she thought. Until the cast came off, she couldn't pitch in any of the softball games coming up. She'd have a hard time doing her schoolwork. "At least I won't have to wash dishes for a while," she grumbled.

But worst of all, the cast meant that Amanda would miss the Recreation Center canoe trip. She'd been looking forward to that adventure for weeks!

"Cheer up, Amanda," her mom said as they got back home. "Four weeks will go by before you know it. And I'll help you any way I can in the meantime."

Amanda slumped down on the couch, sighing. Her cat heard the sigh and strolled over to investigate. Sneakers curled up in Amanda's lap, wrinkling his nose as he sniffed the cast. Amanda laughed. "I can see that you don't like the cast any more than I do," she said. "But there's one thing I can do well right-handed. I can pet you!"

Sneakers purred happily as Amanda did just that.

Complete the Main Idea Worksheet for this story.

© HMH Supplemental Publishers Inc, All rights reserved.

Summarizing Strategies Grade 6, SV 9781419099908

Name _____ Date _____

Main Idea Worksheet

Teacher's
Toolbox

Story Title _____

Complete the Center on the Main Idea diagram based on what you've read.

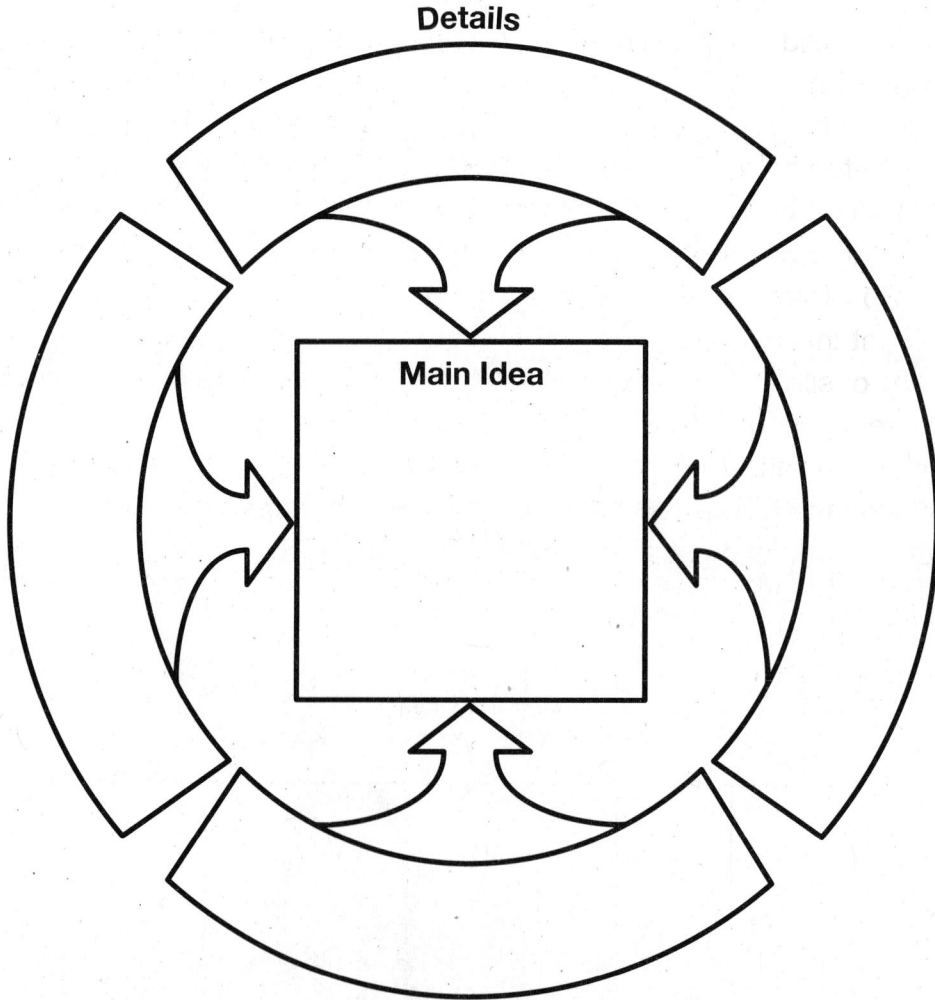

Details

Main Idea

Summary: Use the information in the Center on the Main Idea diagram to write a summary of the reading.

_____

_____

_____

© HMH Supplemental Publishers Inc. All rights reserved.
Summarizing Strategies Grade 6, SV 9781419099908

Supporting Details

Presentation and Model

Strategy: Finding the details that support the main idea

The main idea is the most important idea in what you read. Details give exact information about the main idea. Details support the main idea by answering questions such as: *who, when, where,* or *how.* Good summaries include main ideas and the most important details from the reading.

Read the story below.

Susanna ran from the bus to her house. "Grandma!" she shouted as she slammed the door behind her. "Guess what! I got the part! I'm going to the closet to see what I can wear," Susanna said, rushing off. But a few moments later, she came out of her room looking glum. The pretty dress she had on was too short, too tight—too small! "What am I going to do?" she asked her grandmother. "We don't have money for a new dress."

Grandma stood with her hands on her hips for a moment, examining the dress. "I think I can help," she said. "Go change, and then bring me the dress."

Susanna brought the dress to her grandmother, who sat at her sewing machine. Around her were several yards of silky fabric. Susanna sat on the couch and watched in amazement as her grandmother started working.

"Try this," Grandma said two hours later. Susanna raced to her room, pulled the remade dress over her head, and exclaimed, "My grandmother is a fashion genius!"

Complete the Supporting Pillars diagram based on what you've read.

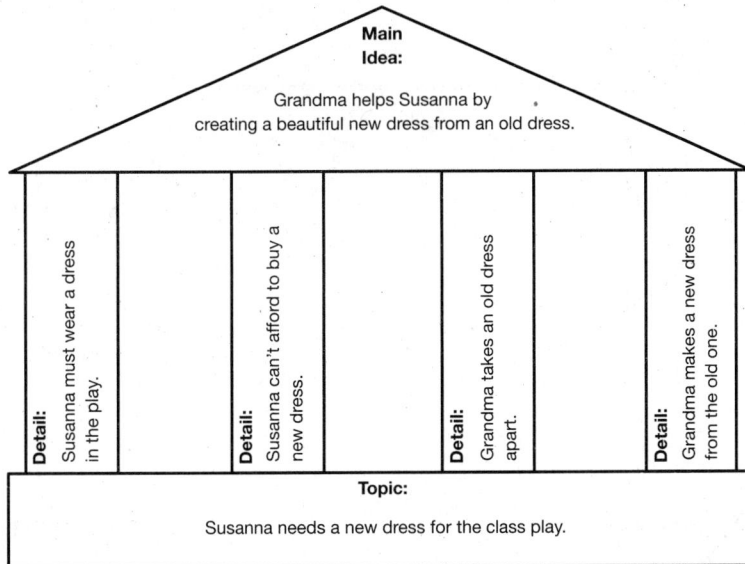

Main Idea:
Grandma helps Susanna by creating a beautiful new dress from an old dress.

Detail: Susanna must wear a dress in the play.

Detail: Susanna can't afford to buy a new dress.

Detail: Grandma takes an old dress apart.

Detail: Grandma makes a new dress from the old one.

Topic:
Susanna needs a new dress for the class play.

Summary: Use the information in the Supporting Pillars diagram to write a summary of the story.

Susanna's concern turns to happiness when her grandmother creatively solves a problem.

Her talented grandmother uses pieces of an old dress and new fabric to make a new dress.

© HMH Supplemental Publishers Inc. All rights reserved.
Summarizing Strategies Grade 6, SV 9781419099908

Supporting Details

Read the article below.

A Quick Note

Handwriting seems to be losing its importance in the world of communication. In the past, it was the primary way for people to share information. At that time, it was very important for people to practice handwriting. Students practiced how to write neat, well-formed letters every day in school.

Today, technology often takes the place of handwriting. Telephones offer instant communication, eliminating the need for many handwritten messages. Computers with e-mail systems are in wide use. Even young students text each other on their cell phones.

But good handwriting is still important. Students need to be able to write clearly and quickly for many reasons. Writing things down can often be more convenient. At other times, a computer or phone may not be available. Students must also take notes and tests in school. Handwritten notes are also more personal. Nice handwriting may not be as important as it once was, but it's still a good skill to develop.

Complete the Supporting Details Worksheet for this article.

© HMH Supplemental Publishers Inc. All rights reserved.

Supporting Details

Read the article below.

Poison Ivy

If you are hiking in the woods, playing at a park, or just helping your family take care of the yard, watch out for poison ivy! How will you know poison ivy when you see it? Just remember this little rhyme: "Leaves of three? Let them be!"

Poison ivy is a common, poisonous plant. It has three leaflets on each stem. Depending on the time of year, it may also have small white berries. Poison ivy can grow as a bush or as a vine. Its leaves are green and shiny in the summer. In the fall, they are a beautiful shade of red.

Some people can have a severe reaction to poison ivy if they come into contact with any part of the plant. The poisonous juice is present in the leaves, stems, and flowers. First, the affected skin gets red and itchy. Then, tiny bumps appear. The reaction can spread on the body and from person to person very easily.

If you do touch poison ivy, do not scratch your skin, no matter how much it itches. Instead, wash the poison off your skin right away. Who knows? Maybe you're one of the lucky people who doesn't react much to poison ivy. But just in case, when you see a plant with "leaves of three," don't take a chance. Stay away from it!

Complete the Supporting Details Worksheet for this article.

© HMH Supplemental Publishers Inc. All rights reserved.
Summarizing Strategies Grade 6, SV 9781419099908

Name _____ Date _____

Supporting Details Worksheet

Story Title _____

Complete the Supporting Pillars diagram based on what you've read.

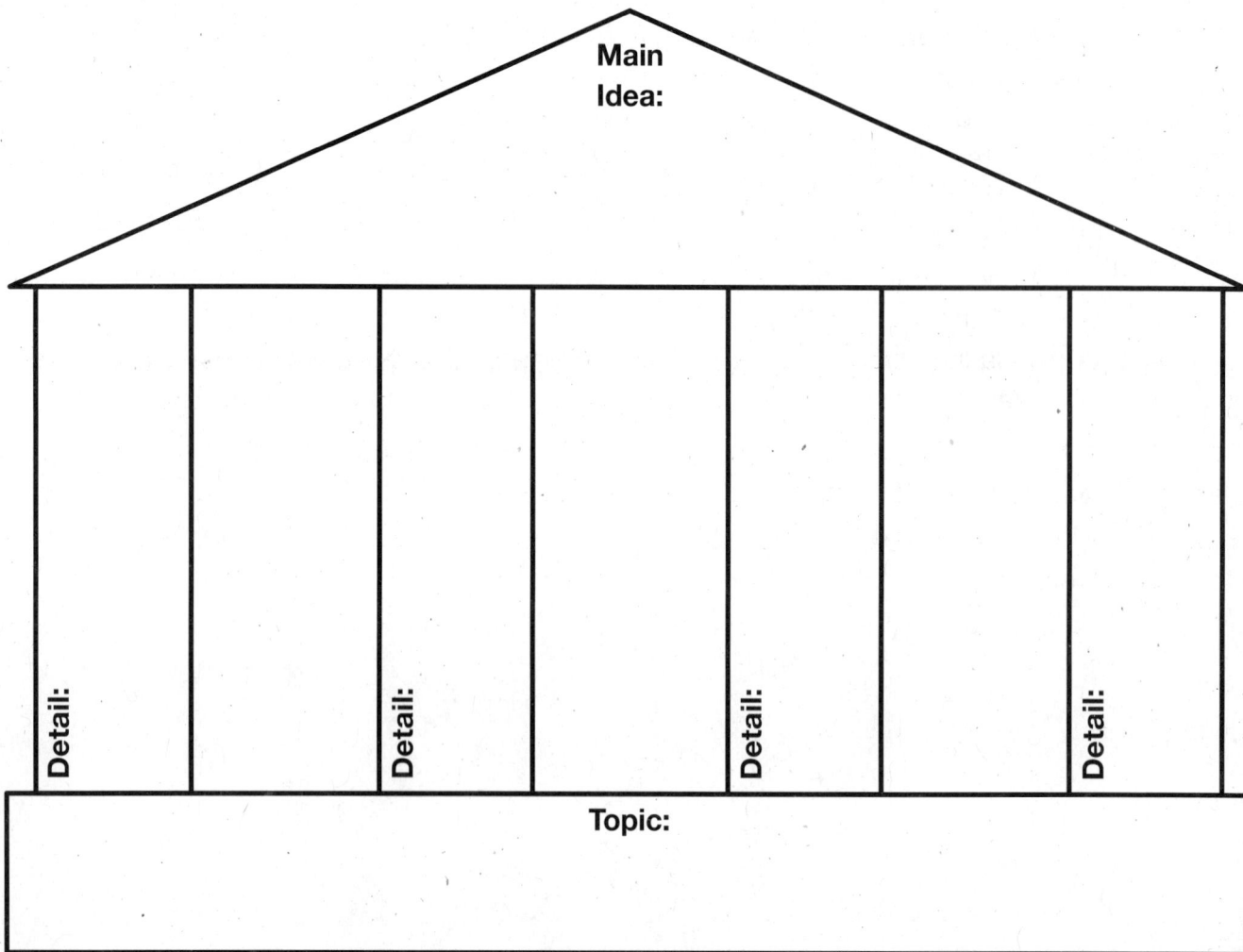

Main Idea:

Detail:

Detail:

Detail:

Detail:

Topic:

Summary: Use the information in the Supporting Pillars diagram to write a summary of the reading.

_____

_____

_____

Creating a Summary

Presentation and Model

Strategy: Summarizing for comprehension and review

When you write a summary, you write a short statement that tells the main facts or events of what you have read. Summaries include only the most important facts. Summarizing is a useful skill, which may help you understand, remember, and study what you have read.

Read the story below.

Carlita had worked with her dad to fix things around the house even before she was old enough for school. She had a natural ability to fix things. Carlita felt proud of her ability, and she was grateful to her dad for teaching her. She had repaired Aunt Jennifer's bike when it was making a horrible grinding sound. When her sister's stereo stopped playing, Carlita tinkered with it for an hour and soon had it working better than ever. Since Carlita had started fixing stuff, not a door or drawer in the house squeaked or stuck.

One day, her father called her to the garage. She hurried outside, eager for a project. "What do you need, Dad?" she said. "Is there something I can help you fix?"

"Not this time, Carlita. I have a surprise for you. I've noticed that you often need to borrow my tools, and sometimes I'm using them when you need them. But today, I'm going to fix that problem." He stepped aside, and Carlita saw a shiny new toolbox sitting on the work table. Carlita smiled in delight and hugged her father. Now she had her very own tools!

Complete the Spoke and Wheel based on what you've read.

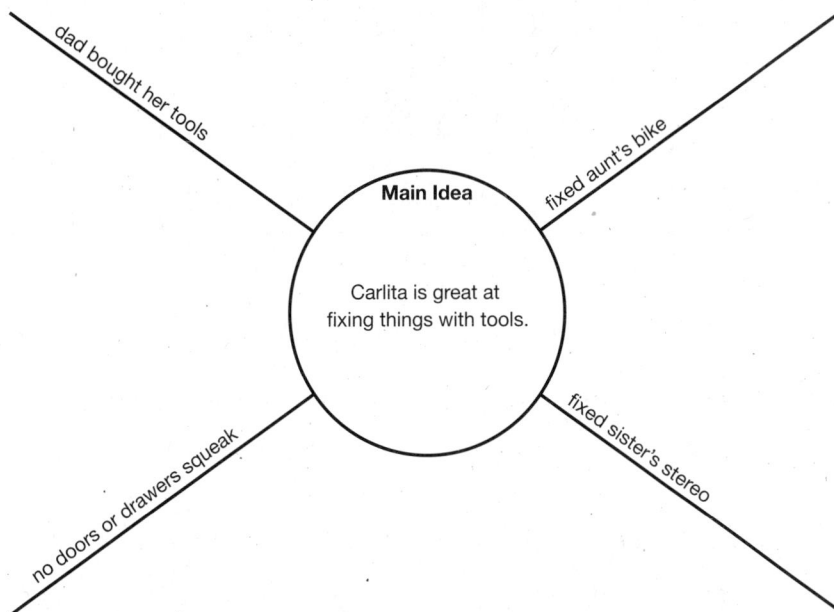

dad bought her tools

fixed aunt's bike

Main Idea

Carlita is great at fixing things with tools.

no doors or drawers squeak

fixed sister's stereo

Summary: Use the information in the Spoke and Wheel to write a summary of the story.

Carlita is very good at fixing things and enjoys doing that kind of work. Her father supports her work by buying her tools of her own.

© HMH Supplemental Publishers Inc. All rights reserved.

Creating a Summary

Read the article below.

A Folk Music Legend

Stephen Foster was an American musician who lived from 1826 to 1864. Foster grew up near Pittsburgh, Pennsylvania. When he was a boy, this area was just east of the nation's frontier. Foster never had the chance to study music or take lessons, but he had a natural gift of capturing the music he heard around him.

Foster composed folk songs such as "My Old Kentucky Home" and "Camptown Races" that were hits in his day and are still played and sung today. He wrote more than 200 songs, in fact.

Though Foster hoped to become a well-known musician and had some success in selling his music, he was not a good businessman. Once he signed a contract to write music for a popular show. The show succeeded, but Foster's name was not on the music. No one knew he had written it until after his death. Foster lived much of his life in debt and died, homeless and almost penniless, when he was just 38 years old.

Complete the Creating a Summary Worksheet for this article.

© HMH Supplemental Publishers Inc. All rights reserved.

Creating a Summary

Read the story below.

Horses, Horses, Horses!

Maria is "horse crazy!" Horses are her favorite subject. Just take a look at her room, and you'll see. She has 27 ceramic horses displayed on a shelf above her bed. Posters of horses are tacked all over her walls. Even her bedspread has horses on it, and she has a horse-shaped pillow!

When Maria has to write a story for school, guess what she writes about—horses! She has written about how she wants a horse of her own, about magical horses that can fly and talk, and about many kinds of real horses. You'll often see her wearing one of her four t-shirts with horses on them. She even named her dog Trigger, after a famous movie horse.

Next summer, Maria will go to a riding camp. She'll learn to take care of horses, from grooming and feeding them to cleaning their stalls. She'll also learn to care for horse tack—saddles, bridles, and so on. She'll get to take her first riding lessons, too. Maria will probably come back from camp more horse-crazy than ever!

Complete the Creating a Summary Worksheet for this story.

© HMH Supplemental Publishers Inc. All rights reserved.

Name _____ Date _____

Creating a Summary Worksheet

Story Title _____

Complete the Spoke and Wheel based on what you've read.

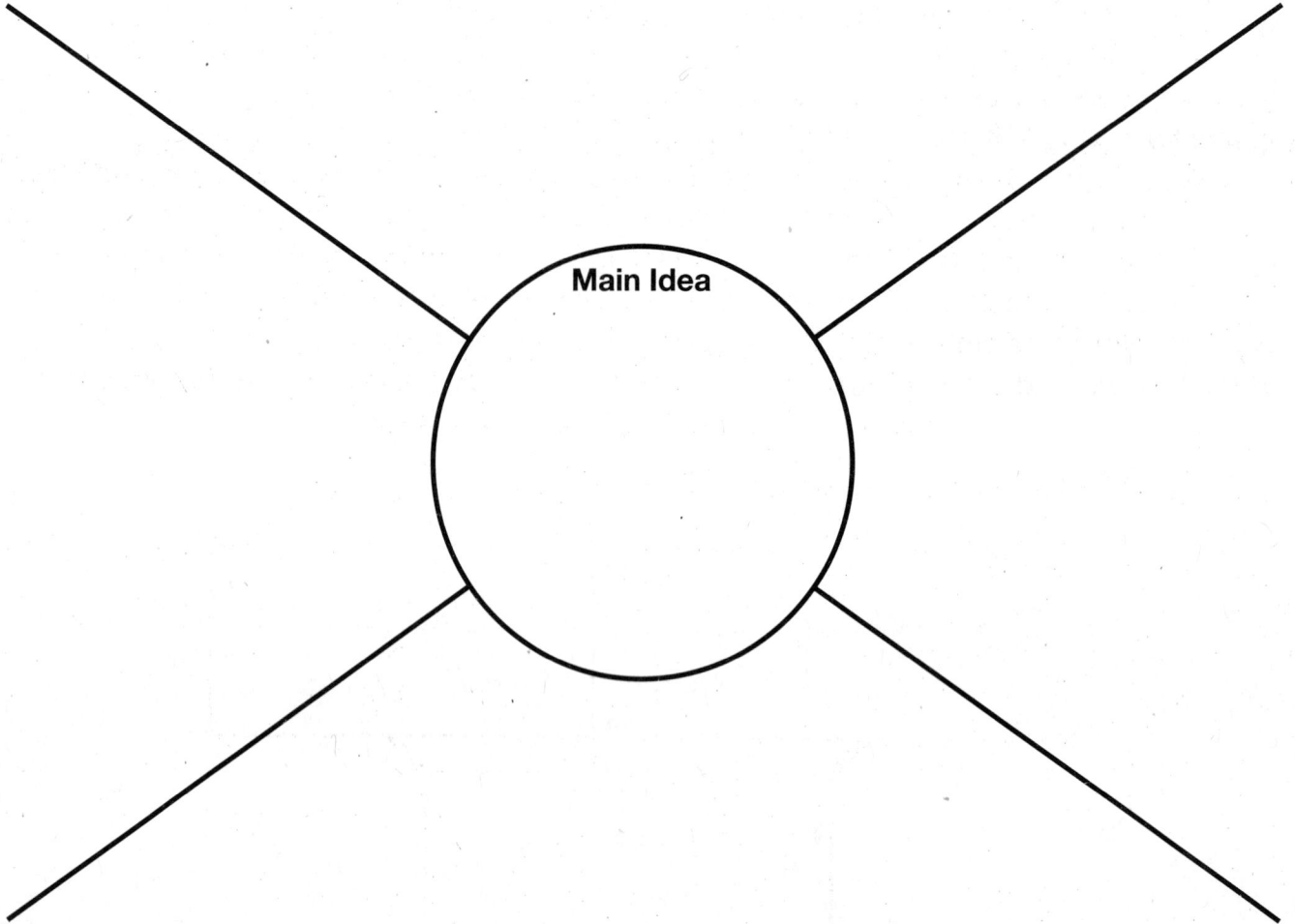

Main Idea

Summary: Use the information in the Spoke and Wheel to write a summary of the reading.

_____

_____

_____

Theme

Presentation and Model

Strategy: Identifying the theme of a story

In works of fiction the overall idea is called the **theme.** The theme is the idea about life or the way people behave that the author wants you to think about.

Read the story below.

"Brenda, we're headed to the park to play soccer. Come with us after you drop off your stuff!" Mai said.

"I can't," Brenda replied. "I have to practice first."

"But it will be dark by the time you're done," Mai complained.

"Go on without me," Brenda said. "I'll try to make it—I promise!" She stepped off the bus. She felt annoyed that she couldn't go to the park. But she was practicing for a music competition. Maybe if she hurried, she could do both.

On most days, Brenda came home from school, had a snack, checked her e-mail, and then practiced. Today, however, she flung her backpack down in the hall and raced to the piano. She set the timer. She had promised her mother that she would practice one hour, and she wanted to keep her promise. Brenda began to work on the song for the competition. The music made her lose track of the time. When the timer went off, she was startled.

Brenda glanced outside. The sun was still up. Quickly, she grabbed her cleats and headed for the park. It felt good to keep her promises, to her mom and to Mai!

Complete the Theme Map based on what you've read.

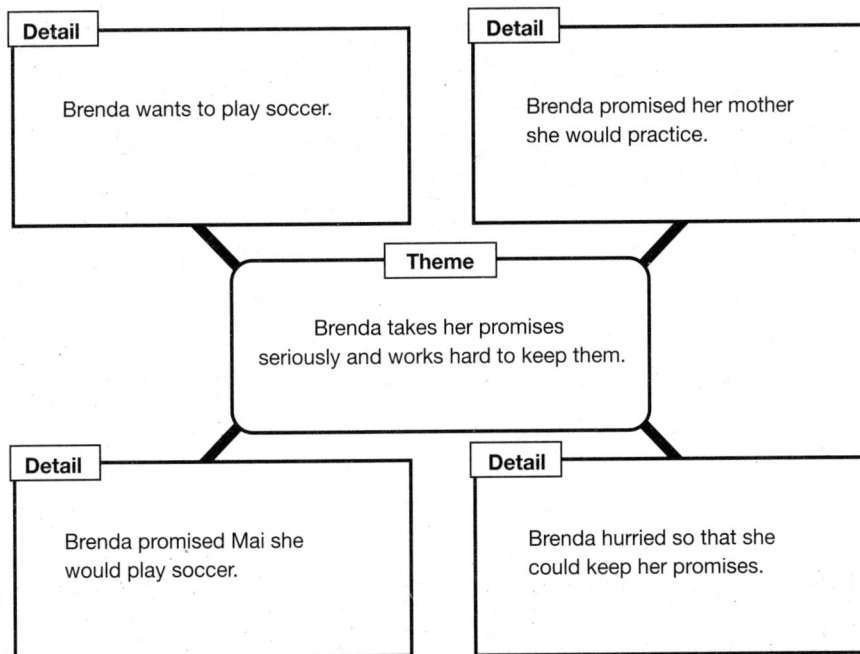

Detail
Brenda wants to play soccer.

Detail
Brenda promised her mother she would practice.

Theme
Brenda takes her promises seriously and works hard to keep them.

Detail
Brenda promised Mai she would play soccer.

Detail
Brenda hurried so that she could keep her promises.

Summary: Use the information in the Theme Map to write a summary of the story.

To Brenda, a promise is something serious to be kept, even if she has to give up something to keep it.

© HMH Supplemental Publishers Inc. All rights reserved.

Theme

Read the story below.

Forgive and Forget

"Marco, are you paying attention?" Mrs. Kelso asked sharply. "This is the fifth time I've had to call your name. You and Stan seem to be out of touch today."

Marco glared across his desk at Stan. Stan glared back. Both ignored the teacher. They were too angry to pay attention.

At lunch, Marco made a point of sitting at a table far away from Stan's, but not so far away that he couldn't continue to throw angry glances at him. Stan, for his part, made a point of turning his back on Marco. At recess, the boys chunked basketballs through hoops at the opposite ends of the court.

Finally, Jay tossed the ball to Marco and said, "What is up with you and Stan? You two are behaving weirdly! I thought you were best friends."

Marco said, "Stan's a jerk! Let me tell you what he did this morning." As he started to complain about Stan, Marco realized that he couldn't remember why he was so angry. What had Stan said on the bus earlier? Whatever it was, it started this fight. Now the fight was becoming more important than their friendship.

"You know, you're right, Jay. Stan is my best friend, but I'm not acting like his best friend." He grabbled a ball and ran, dribbling it, to the other end of the court. One way or another, he was going to get back on good terms with his friend.

Complete the Theme Worksheet for this story.

© HMH Supplemental Publishers Inc. All rights reserved.
Summarizing Strategies Grade 6, SV 9781419099908

Theme

Read the story below.

The Big Surprise

Lena's birthday party with her family began as usual. First, the Rodriguez family gathered in the living room after dinner. Several colorfully wrapped presents sat on the rug. Lena was excited to open them, even though she already knew what was in them. Her parents had never been able to surprise her!

After Lena opened one gift—the new CD she'd been expecting—she heard a faint rustling noise. She paused to listen for a moment but didn't hear anything else. She reached for another present. All of a sudden, the present moved! Lena sprang to her feet in alarm.

Laughing, Lena's father picked up the moving present. The box had no bottom at all. Beneath it was a fluffy white kitten. It had been batting at the sides of the box. Lena was so surprised! She couldn't decide which was better—the gift, or the fact that she had no idea what was in the box.

Complete the Theme Worksheet for this story.

© HMH Supplemental Publishers Inc. All rights reserved.
Summarizing Strategies Grade 6, SV 9781419099908

Name _____   Date _____

Teacher's Toolbox

Theme Worksheet

Story Title _____

Complete the Theme Map based on what you've read.

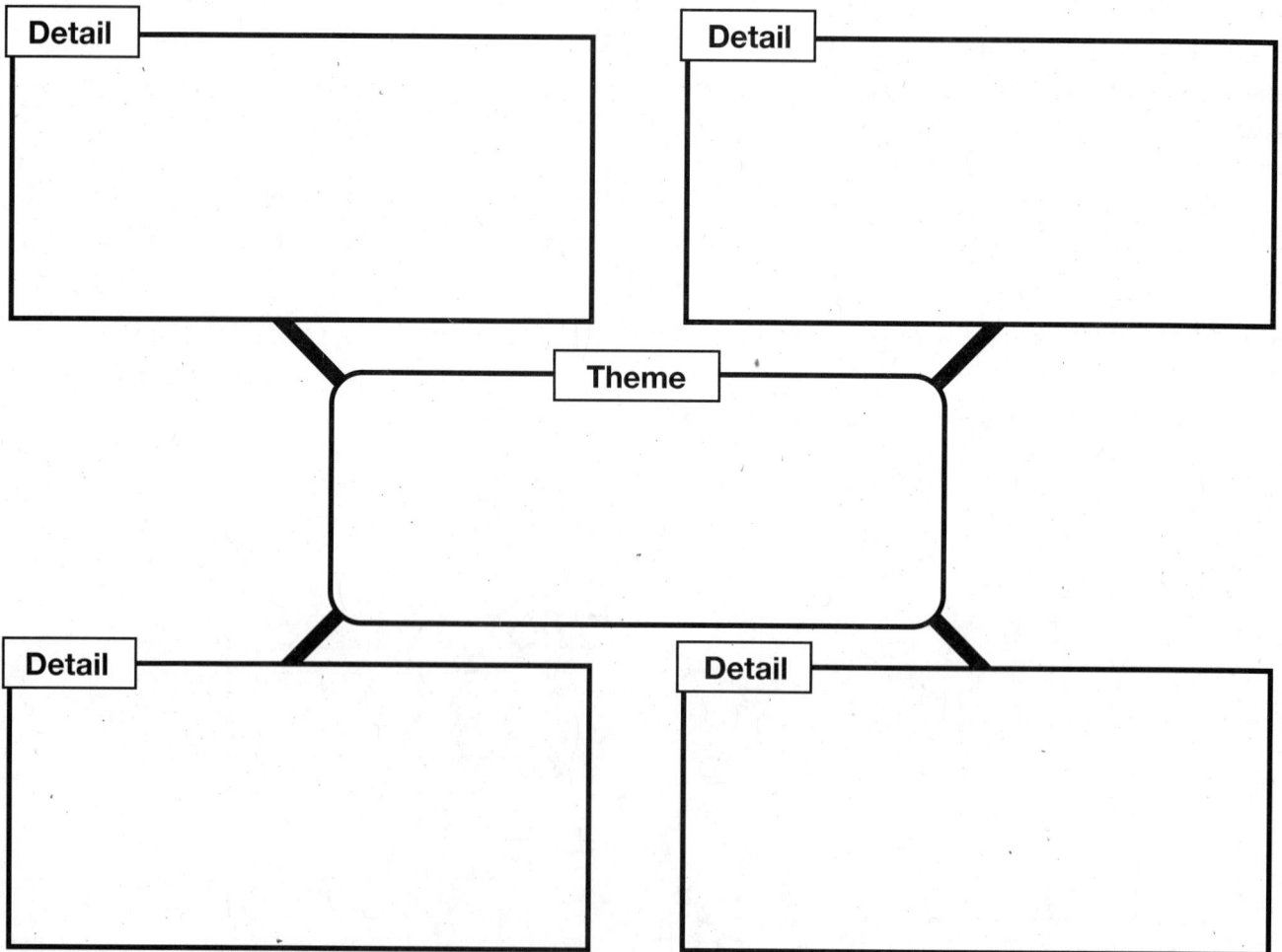

Detail	Detail

Theme

Detail	Detail

Summary: Use the information in the Theme Map to write a summary of the reading.

_____

_____

_____

© HMH Supplemental Publishers Inc. All rights reserved.

Compare and Contrast

Presentation and Model

Strategy: Comparing and contrasting information that you read

When you compare, you look for how things are alike. When you contrast, you look for how things are different. Comparing and contrasting can help you organize what you read.

Read the article below.

If you've ever visited an art museum, you know that artists use a variety of materials when they create their works. Painters, for example, use watercolors or oils to create pictures. They may paint on canvas or directly on walls. A painter needs brushes, rags, and sponges in his or her studio.

Sculptors, on the other hand, need very different kinds of materials. Some sculptors work with rocks, even with massive stones. They shape the stones to create art. Some use a pottery wheel to shape clay, which they then bake and decorate. Other sculptors work in metals, first making small models and then using fire to melt metal into a larger work. These artists often need large workshops and heavy tools to do their work.

Still other artists create art out of whatever they find. We call this kind of art "mixed media." Mixed media artists might use things found in nature, such as rocks, grasses, or clays. Some even use trash or items they find lying around to make interesting, unexpected works of art. You never know what you will see in this kind of art.

Complete the Compare-Contrast Chart based on what you've read.

How Topics Are Alike		How Topics Are Different
They create interesting art. You might see their art in museums. Each needs certain materials and tools to create art.	**Topic 1:** Painters	Painters use oils, watercolors, and brushes. They paint on canvasses or walls.
	Topic 2: Sculptors	Sculptors use clay, stone, and metal. They may need fire and heavy tools to create their art.
	Topic 3: Mixed media artists	Mixed media artists use all kinds of things found in nature and even in the trash to create their art.

Summary: Use the information in the Compare-Contrast Chart to write a summary of the article.

Many kinds of artists create works of art for museums. Painters, sculptors, and mixed media

artists work with different materials and tools to create their art works.

Compare and Contrast

Read the article below.

Wasps—Busy as Bees

The Elvis Crawford Nature Center recently hosted a lecture by Dr. Whitfield. She is an expert on wasps. Many of the people in attendance were surprised to hear about the number of types of wasps there are.

Dr. Whitfield pointed out that although many people are afraid of wasps, they are actually helpful to people and nature. Wasps pollinate flowers and crops. Wasps eat pests that destroy crops. However, wasps can sting, so people should be cautious around them. Most wasps would rather avoid people than sting them, fortunately.

Dr. Whitfield explained that wasps build various kinds of nests. The paper wasp, for example, builds a nest out of paper. Yellow jackets, on the other hand, build large nests in the ground. The potter wasp builds a little jug-like nest on a twig. Dr. Whitfield showed several pictures of these nests. Many of the photographs had very complex nests. Some people thought that the potter wasp's nest looked almost as if a person had made it and then stuck it on the twig.

Complete the Compare and Contrast Worksheet for this article.

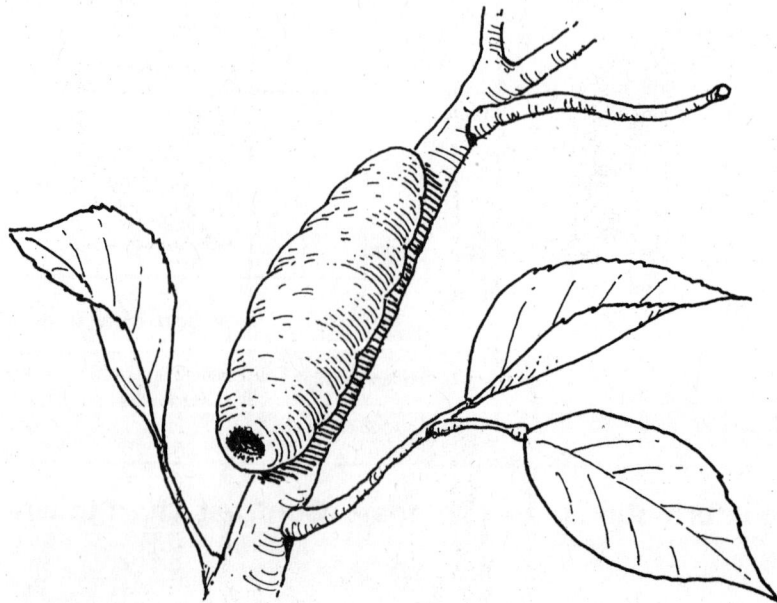

© HMH Supplemental Publishers Inc. All rights reserved.

Summarizing Strategies Grade 6, SV 9781419099908

Compare and Contrast

Read the story below.

Roger's Collections

No one would doubt that Roger likes to collect things. When he was little, he collected pebbles and sticks that he found outside. Now that he's older, he is working on three serious collections.

First, he collects stamps. He has stamps that are old and stamps that are new. He has stamps from many countries. Roger uses a web site to trade stamps so that his collection is always growing. He stores the stamps carefully in a notebook.

Second, Roger collects baseball cards. He is just getting started with this collection, but he wants to earn money to buy some rare cards rather than buying lots of common cards. He has one card that is very special. It is in a frame hanging above his desk.

Finally, Roger collects coins. His coin collection is already pretty large because his grandparents helped him build it. They had coins from when they were young, and they added these to the collections. Roger examines the coins carefully and learns about their value from books.

Roger hopes that his collections will become more valuable over time. He certainly takes good care of them.

Complete the Compare and Contrast Worksheet for this story.

© HMH Supplemental Publishers Inc. All rights reserved.

Name _____ Date _____

Teacher's
Toolbox

Compare and Contrast Worksheet

Story Title _____

Complete the Compare-Contrast Chart based on what you've read.

How Topics Are Alike		How Topics Are Different
	Topic 1:	
	Topic 2:	
	Topic 3:	

Summary: Use the information in the Compare-Contrast Chart to write a summary of the reading.

_____

_____

_____

Story Map

Presentation and Model

Strategy: Outlining the plot of a story

You can summarize a story's plot by outlining what happens during its beginning, middle, and end. When you know a plot's outline, you have a basic understanding of the story.

Read the story below.

What a decision to have to make! Nikki gazed out the window, missing the end of the movie on TV, because she couldn't think of anything else. The spring school break was coming up, and she had been so excited. Her best friend's family had invited her to go skiing with them. Nikki had never been skiing before. Now was her chance!

But today Nikki's parents told her that her grandmother was coming to visit during the break. Mimi lived in another state, and travel was hard for her. She wouldn't be coming to visit again for a long time. Nikki loved Mimi and wanted to see her.

"Maybe Mom and Dad will make me stay home," she had thought. "Then I won't have to choose."

But her parents wanted Nikki to decide. "You won't get a chance to go skiing for a very long time," they said. "You should think about it."

As Nikki stared out the window, the phone rang. Sharon was on the line. "Nikki, you know that you're my best friend," she began, "and I really want you to go skiing with us. But I know how much you want to see your grandmother. My parents say that you can go to the mountains with us another time. So stay and have a great visit!"

As Nikki hung up, she thought about how lucky she was to have such a great friend.

Complete the Plot Sequence Chart based on what you've read.

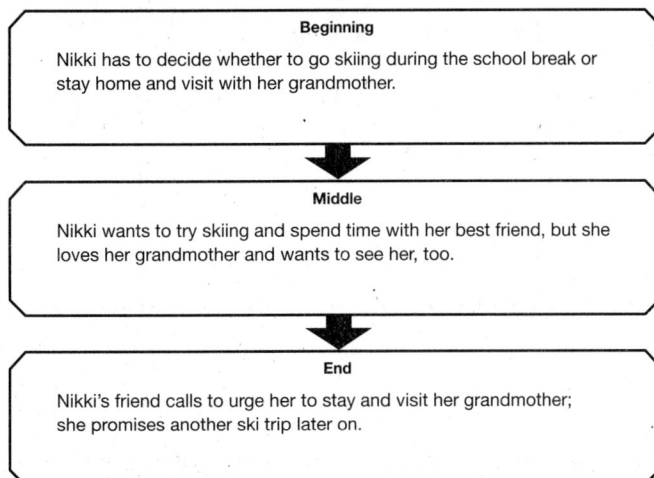

Beginning

Nikki has to decide whether to go skiing during the school break or stay home and visit with her grandmother.

⬇

Middle

Nikki wants to try skiing and spend time with her best friend, but she loves her grandmother and wants to see her, too.

⬇

End

Nikki's friend calls to urge her to stay and visit her grandmother; she promises another ski trip later on.

Summary: Use the information in the Plot Sequence Chart to write a summary of the story.

Nikki is torn about how to spend her school break, but her best friend helps her make

a decision that they both feel good about.

Story Map

Read the story below.

JoJo Has the Jitters

After months of making promises, James finally got his hamster. He'd wanted one for a long time. His cousin Ramiro had two hamsters, and they were fun to play with.

James had promised to feed his hamster, JoJo, to clean his cage, and to keep him away from the family dog. Now, at last, JoJo was in the habitat in James's bedroom. "Fantastic!" James thought.

About midnight, however, James began to wonder how fantastic having a hamster would be. JoJo was so noisy! Digging through his bedding, gnawing on a chewy toy, running in his wheel—the noise made it hard for James to sleep. The next morning, when James fed JoJo, the hamster felt scared and nipped his finger! James was beginning to regret his promises. But his mother said, "I'm sorry, James, but you wanted a hamster, and now you've got one. You can't take him back."

Later that day, Ramiro came over to meet the hamster. "So, how was last night?" he asked, grinning slyly. James listed all of the problems in disgust. "I know, I know," said Ramiro. "That happened to me, too, at first. Here's what you do: put a towel over JoJo's cage at night. Also, oil his wheel. And give him time to settle down. He's nervous in his new home, but he'll feel better and more playful later."

James felt a little better. Maybe having a hamster would be fun after all!

Complete the Story Map Worksheet for this story.

© HMH Supplemental Publishers Inc. All rights reserved.

Summarizing Strategies Grade 6, SV 9781419099908

Story Map

Read the story below.

Ned and the Noise

Nervously, Ned crossed the hall to his parents' bedroom door. He tapped quietly. "Mom? Dad? Are you awake?" he whispered loudly.

"Well, we are now, Ned. Is something wrong?" his dad asked.

"I heard noises. I think someone's outside the window!" Ned said, feeling a little silly, but scared, too.

"I'll come check it out. Just a minute," Dad said.

Soon the door opened and Dad walked out. "What did you hear?" asked Dad.

"It sounded like glass breaking," Ned explained. "But it's windy out, so maybe I just heard the wind." He felt bad for waking up his father.

"Let's check, just to be sure." Dad toured the house, checking each window. Everything seemed fine. "Maybe it was the window in the shed," he said. With flashlight in hand, he led Ned out back. A few steps from the door, the beam of light glinted off broken glass in the next yard. "Oh, here's what you heard," Dad said. "It looks like a branch hit the window of the empty house next door."

As they said good night in the hall, Ned felt embarrassed about having been scared. But Dad said, "Thanks for helping me keep an eye on things around here, Ned. Good work!"

Complete the Story Map Worksheet for this story.

© HMH Supplemental Publishers Inc. All rights reserved.

Summarizing Strategies Grade 6, SV 9781419099908

Story Map Worksheet

Teacher's Toolbox

Story Title _____

Complete the Plot Sequence Chart based on what you've read.

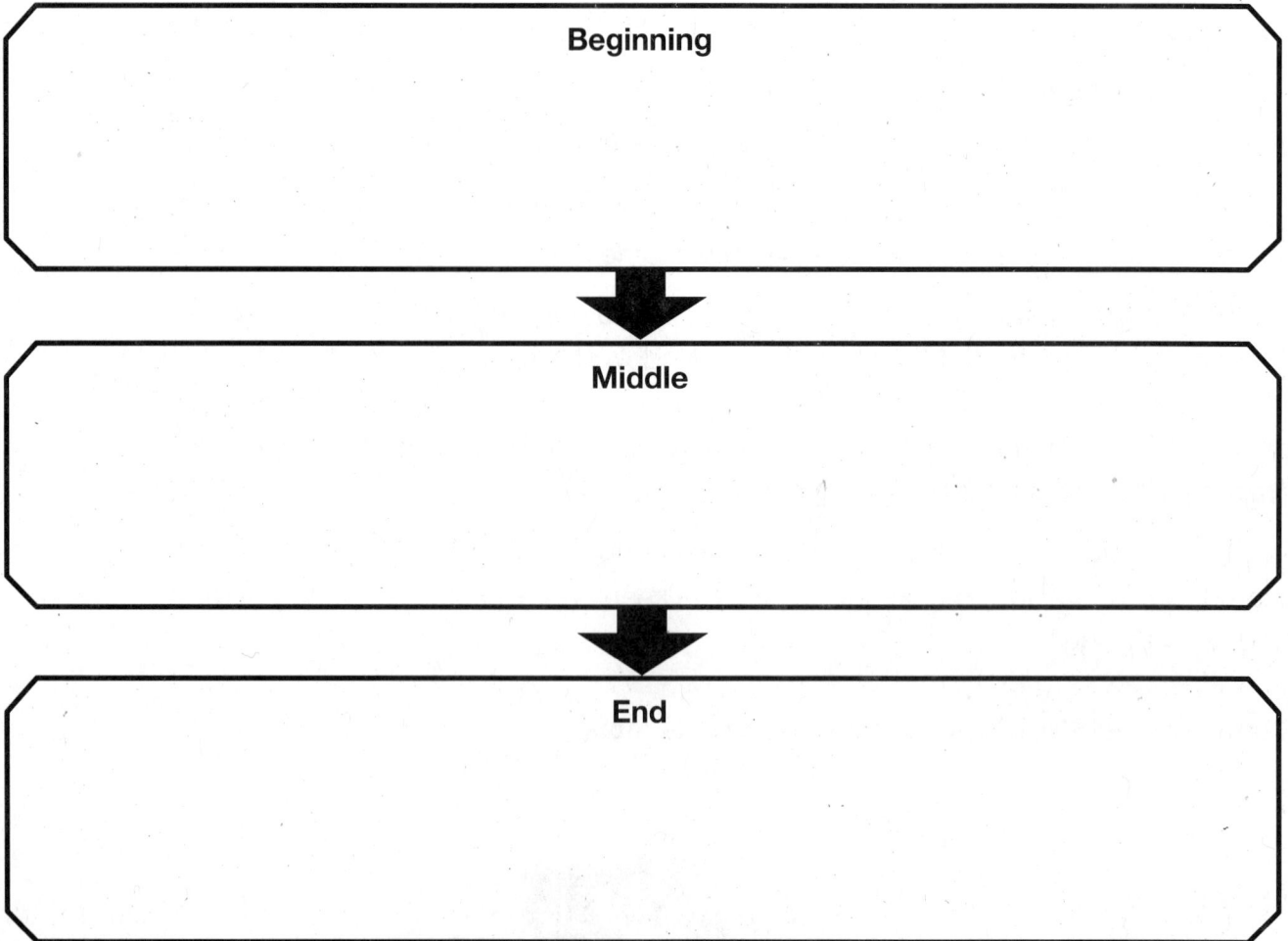

Beginning

⬇

Middle

⬇

End

Summary: Use the information in the Plot Sequence Chart to write a summary of the reading.

_____

_____

_____

Understanding Graphics

Presentation and Model

Strategy: Summarizing information presented in graphics

Not all information is presented in nicely written paragraphs. Sometimes you will see information presented in graphs, charts, checklists, or tables. You can summarize this information, too.

Study the survey results below.

Violanda wanted to find out what the recycling habits were of her community. She walked around her neighborhood and asked an adult at each house whether they recycled, and if so did they recycle paper, plastic, or both.

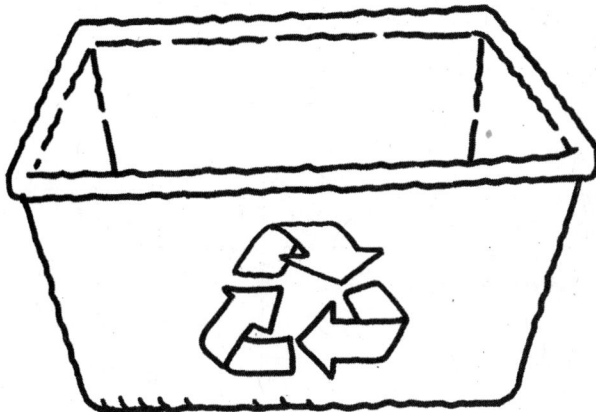

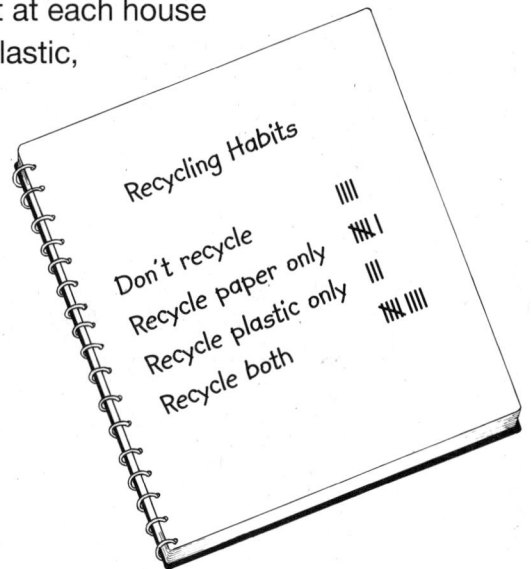

Recycling Habits

Don't recycle   IIII

Recycle paper only   T111 I

Recycle plastic only   III

Recycle both   T111 IIII

Complete the Q Matrix based on what you've read.

	Don't recycle	Paper only	Plastic only	Both
How many?	4	6	3	9
Most common?				✓
Least common?			✓	

Summary: Use the information in the Q Matrix to write a summary of the survey.

Of the 22 houses surveyed in the neighborhood, the most houses recycle both paper and plastic. When you add paper only together with paper and plastic, more than half recycle at least paper.

© HMH Supplemental Publishers Inc. All rights reserved.

Understanding Graphics

Study the survey results below.

New Book Order

It was time for Williams Elementary to order some new books for the library. The librarians thought it would be a good idea to keep track of what types of books the students most often checked out over a two-day period. That would let them know what kinds of books to order.

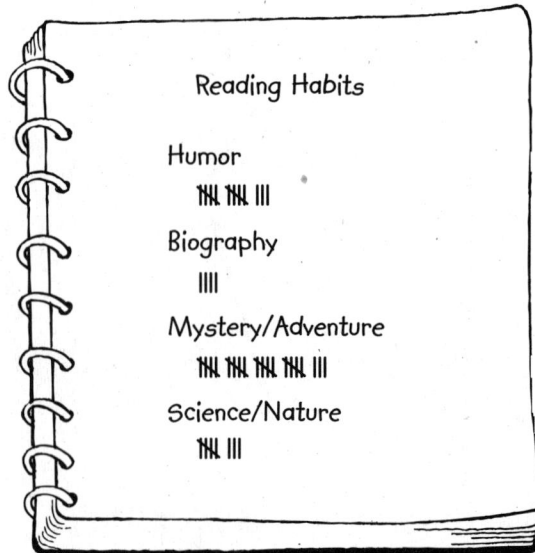

Reading Habits

Humor
|||| |||| |||

Biography
||||

Mystery/Adventure
|||| |||| |||| |||| |||

Science/Nature
|||| |||

Complete the Understanding Graphics Worksheet for this survey.

© HMH Supplemental Publishers Inc. All rights reserved.

Understanding Graphics

Study the survey results below.

Where Should We Go?

As the sixth grade teachers tried to decide where to take their spring field trip, they decided to find out what the students might like to see. The teachers chose four fun spots and let the children vote.

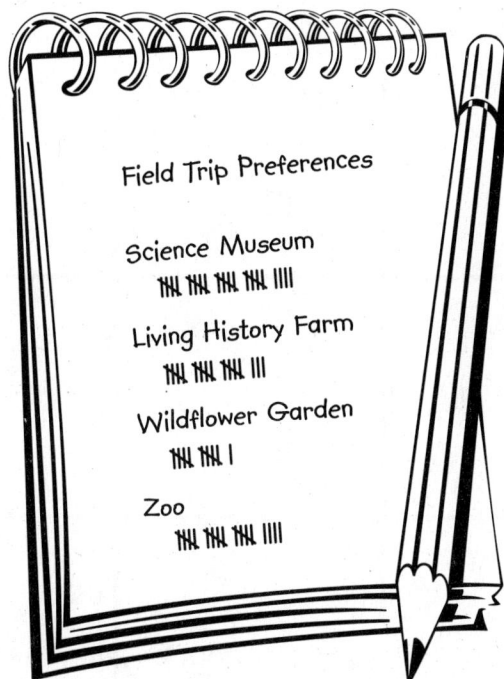

Field Trip Preferences

Science Museum
卌 卌 卌 卌 IIII

Living History Farm
卌 卌 卌 III

Wildflower Garden
卌 卌 I

Zoo
卌 卌 卌 IIII

Complete the Understanding Graphics Worksheet for this story.

© HMH Supplemental Publishers Inc. All rights reserved.
Summarizing Strategies Grade 6, SV 9781419099908

Understanding Graphics Worksheet

Teacher's
Toolbox

Story Title _____

Complete the Q Matrix based on what you've read.

Summary: Use the information in the Q Matrix to write a summary of the survey.

_____

_____

_____

Problems and Solutions

Presentation and Model

Strategy: Identifying problems and solutions in what you read

You will sometimes read paragraphs that talk about a problem and suggest solutions. Sometimes the problem is complicated, and many possible solutions are offered. You will need to study the problem and solution(s) carefully before you can summarize them.

Read the story below.

One rainy Saturday, Marla and her brother Dylan sat looking out the window. They'd played every rainy day game they knew, but the rain kept falling. They'd read books for a while, hoping that the rain would let up. They were bored.

"Well, I guess we can watch TV for a while," Dylan said. But a quick scan of the channels showed that nothing interesting was on.

"I can't believe that not even one good movie is on!" complained Marla. Then she had a brainstorm. "I know! Let's make our own movie!"

Marla and Dylan thought up a silly plot, gathered clothes for costumes, and found some funny props. Then they got the family's video camera and went to work.

After dinner, Dylan announced to the family, "We have a surprise for you! Everyone please come to the den." Marla grabbed a big bowl of popcorn and followed. Then the children debuted their masterpiece: *The Rainy-Day Riddle.*

Complete the Bright Idea graphic based on what you've read.

Problem

Marla and Dylan are bored on a rainy day.

Solution

Marla and Dylan have fun making a home movie.

Summary: Use the information in the Bright Idea graphic to write a summary of the story.

On a rainy day, Marla and Dylan fight boredom by making up a mystery and filming it with a

video camera.

© HMH Supplemental Publishers Inc. All rights reserved.

Problems and Solutions

Read the story below.

The Clubhouse

"I wish we had a place to play," sighed Leia.

"We could go to the park," Matt suggested.

"No, I mean a special place—a place all our own," Leia explained. "Maybe a tree house or a clubhouse."

"Brilliant! Let's ask my grandpa if we can build a clubhouse near his shed!"

Matt's grandfather was happy to let the kids build a clubhouse. He even helped them plan it. "First," he said, "you'll need some wood and nails. I've got some stuff left over from when I built the shed, so let's see what's there."

Before long, word spread, and kids from the whole block were helping to build the clubhouse, as Matt's grandpa supervised them. The clubhouse went up quicker than the kids expected.

"This is great!" Leia said. "But it's kind of dull looking."

"Not for long," announced her neighbor Bryan. "My mom gave me the paint left over from our house. It's blue and green."

Painting the clubhouse was even more fun than building it. The kids thanked Matt's grandpa. They were proud of their new place!

Complete the Problems and Solutions Worksheet for this story.

© HMH Supplemental Publishers Inc. All rights reserved.
Summarizing Strategies Grade 6, SV 9781419099908

Problems and Solutions

Read the story below.

Jason's Pile of Homework

Jason sighed as he set his books on the kitchen table. He got out his math and checked his assignment log. His teacher had assigned many math problems to work. Jason noticed that he also had a chapter to read in his science book. That would take about half an hour. Jason frowned as he remembered that he had to write a paragraph about his favorite sport for English, too.

"This is going to take all evening to do!" he complained. "I'll be lucky if I have time to sleep!"

Jason's mom overheard him. She came and sat down at the table. "How can I help?" she asked.

"You can't," Jason said. "No one can. I just have to sit here and do all of this."

"Yes, you do have to do the work, but maybe I can help make it more pleasant. First, I'll make sure that no one disturbs you, and I'll ask your sister to turn the TV way down. Second, I'll make you a plate of power snacks."

"What are power snacks?" asked Jason.

"Oh, cheese and crackers, an apple, cold water—food to keep you thinking clearly. You get started, and I'll be back soon."

Jason looked at his homework with new eyes. Now he felt that he could do it all, and do it well.

Complete the Problems and Solutions Worksheet for this story.

© HMH Supplemental Publishers Inc. All rights reserved.
Summarizing Strategies Grade 6, SV 9781419099908

Name _____ Date _____

Teacher's Toolbox

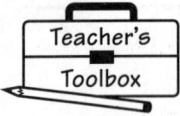

Problems and Solutions Worksheet

Story Title _____

Complete the Bright Idea graphic based on what you've read.

Solution

Problem

Summary: Use the information in the Bright Idea graphic to write a summary of the reading.

_____

_____

_____

© HMH Supplemental Publishers Inc. All rights reserved.

Plot

Presentation and Model

Strategy: Writing a clear plot summary of a story

The series of events in a story can be grouped together and called the plot. The plot explains the questions: *what, why,* and *how?* Answering these questions will give you a summary of what a story is about.

Read the story below.

When Katie moved to Florida, she bought a house with a nice kitchen, two bedrooms, and a den. The layout was perfect for her cats Flower and Louie to run and play in. They especially loved to sit on the windowsill.

On the day Katie moved in, Flower and Louie had fun leaping from carton to carton, pulling out packing paper, and hiding between layers of clothing still packed in boxes. Flower and Louie were thrilled with this game.

Katie finished unpacking just as rain began to fall. As she closed the last drawer, she wondered where the cats were. Flower was sprawled on the bed, but Louie was nowhere in sight. Katie checked under the sink and behind the sofa, but couldn't find Louie anywhere.

Katie began to worry. Did Louie slip out the door? Maybe he was in a box that had been carried out to the trash! She dashed outside and checked the empty boxes—no cat! As she came back into the house, Katie heard a faint meow. She went to the dresser and opened the drawer. Out jumped Louie, lost no more!

Complete the Plot Pie Chart based on what you've read.

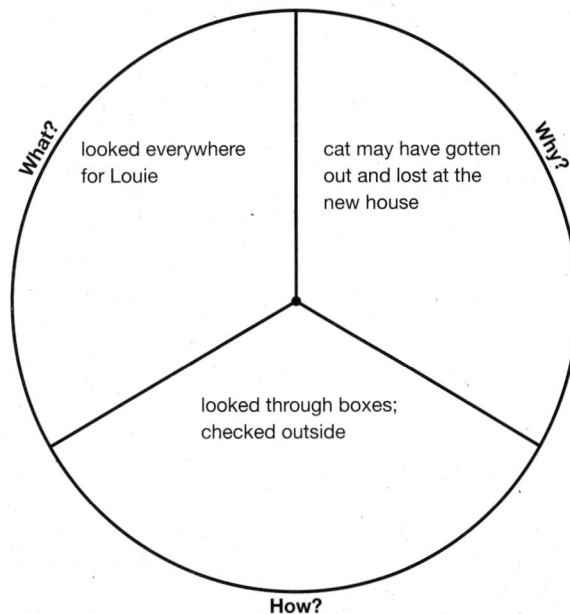

What? looked everywhere for Louie

Why? cat may have gotten out and lost at the new house

How? looked through boxes; checked outside

Summary: Use the information in the Plot Pie Chart to write a summary of the story.

Katie's adventurous cat Louie hides in a drawer that she then closes. She searches

frantically for him until she hears his meow from the drawer.

Plot

Read the story below.

The Fox's Tale

A fox had the misfortune to get his bushy tail caught in a trap. When he saw that it was a question of his life or his tail, he left the tail behind. He felt disgraced, however, and for a time he did not go near his friends for fear of ridicule.

But one day the idea came to him how he could make the best of the situation. He called a meeting of all the rest of the foxes and proposed to them that they should follow his example.

"You have no idea," he said, "of the ease and comfort I am enjoying. I don't know why I didn't cut off my tail long ago. I could never have believed it if I had not tried it myself. When you come to think of it, friends, a tail is such an inconvenient and unnecessary appendage that it is strange we have put up with it so long. My sincere advice to you all is to share this new freedom and part with your tails at once."

As he concluded, one of the older and wiser foxes stepped forward and said, "There is not one of us who does not believe that you found it convenient to cut off your tail. However, we are not so convinced that you would advise us to part with our tails if there were any chance of recovering your own."

Complete the Plot Worksheet for this story.

© HMH Supplemental Publishers Inc. All rights reserved.
Summarizing Strategies Grade 6, SV 9781419099908

Plot

Read the story below.

Lost and Found

"This is fun," shouted Juliet to Tanya. Both girls were spinning as fast as they could, twirling in circles until they were so dizzy that they couldn't stand up. Then they lay in the yard, feeling that the earth was swinging about under them. "Let's do it again!"

The girls were out of breath with excitement and laughter when Tanya suddenly gasped. Her hand was at her throat. "My necklace—the necklace Aunt Amy gave me—it's gone!" she cried. Tears came into her eyes, because the necklace was special to her. Then she thought of what her aunt would say.

"Go get your dad. He'll help you look for it," said Juliet. They looked in dismay at the thick grass and tall bushes in the yard.

"I'll bet he'll just get mad at me," Tanya said, but she went inside to find him anyway.

To her surprise, her father was not angry. "Accidents happen, Tanya, but you should be more careful in the future. You can't wear a fragile necklace when you're playing so hard."

Dad brought a funny-looking device into the yard. It beeped and hummed. "This is a metal detector. It will help us find anything metal hidden in the grass."

It didn't take long to find the necklace. "Thanks, Dad," Julia said. She hugged him gratefully. "I won't let that happen again."

Complete the Plot Worksheet for this story.

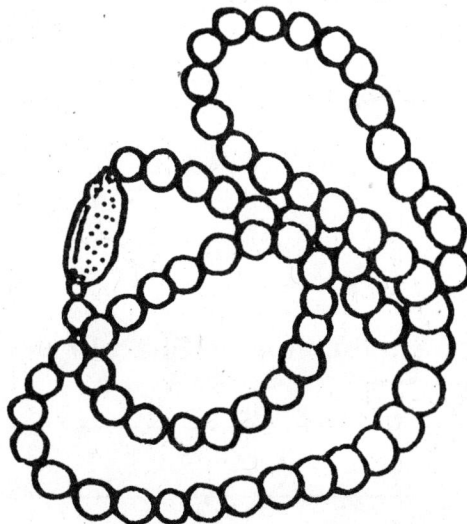

© HMH Supplemental Publishers Inc. All rights reserved.

Summarizing Strategies Grade 6, SV 9781419099908

Name _____ Date _____

Plot Worksheet

Teacher's Toolbox

Story Title _____

Complete the Plot Pie Chart based on what you've read.

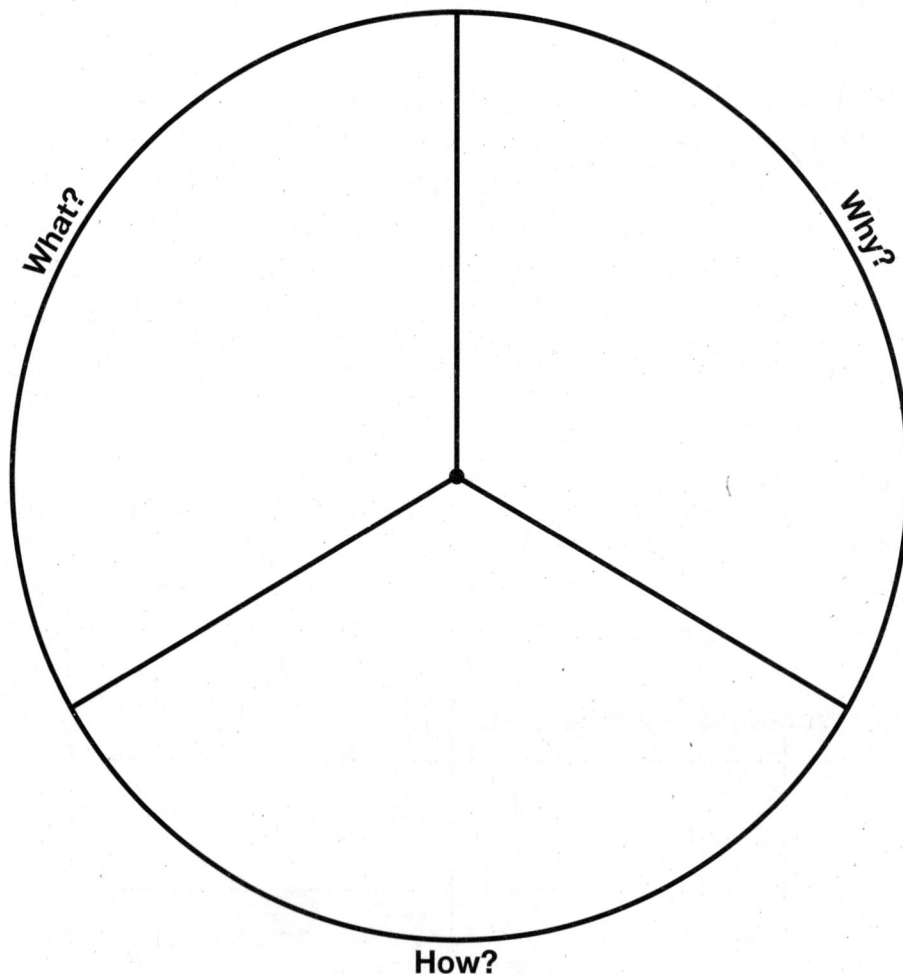

What?

Why?

How?

Summary: Use the information in the Plot Pie Chart to write a summary of the reading.

_____

_____

_____

www.harcourtschoolsupply.com
© HMH Supplemental Publishers Inc. All rights reserved.

Plot
Summarizing Strategies Grade 6, SV 9781419099908

Character's Motivation

Presentation and Model

Strategy: Understanding why characters do what they do

A motivation is a reason for doing something. Analyzing motivations can help you summarize a story. A character's motivation may build suspense, make you laugh, or teach you something.

Read the story below.

Philippe yawned and stretched. He forced his eyes to look at the bright sunlight coming through the window. "Ten more days" was his first thought upon waking up. In fact, the countdown to his 12th birthday was the first thing on his mind every day when he woke up. The day he turned 12 would be a special day indeed.

Philippe's father was a woodworker, one of the best in their part of France. Noblemen paid his father to build furniture for their homes, and once he had been asked to make and carve beautiful doors for a cathedral. Philippe remembered running his fingers across the carefully carved vines and grapes in the dark, spicy-smelling wood.

Papa noted Philippe's interest in woodworking with pleasure. He let Philippe help him in small ways, carrying wood and sweeping shavings. But he would not let Philippe touch the precious woodworking tools. If they were to break, how would the family make its living?

But in 10 more days, just 10, Philippe would be old enough to begin learning his father's trade. He swung his legs over the edge of his bed and got up to dress. How, he wondered, might he be able to help his father today?

Complete the Character Motivation Table based on what you've read.

Character's name: Philippe

	Action	Motivation
1.	He thinks about the number of days until his birthday.	He is excited to turn 12 so that he can begin to work with wood.
2.	He runs his fingers across the carved doors.	He appreciates the beauty of the wood and the hard work his papa has done.
3.	He carries wood and sweeps shavings.	He wants to help in the shop any way he can.
4.	He wonders how he can help his papa today.	He wants to show that he is ready to learn to work with wood.

Summary: Use the information in the Character Motivation Table to write a summary of the story.

Philippe can't wait to turn 12 so that he can start carving wood with his father. Until his

birthday, he is happy to do other jobs around the shop.

© HMH Supplemental Publishers Inc. All rights reserved.

Character's Motivation

Read the story below.

The Best Neighbors Around

Mrs. Johnson always baked cookies for new people in her neighborhood. She listened to children when they asked her questions and tried to help them if they had a problem. She always offered a helping hand if she knew that someone might need it.

One day, the people in Mrs. Johnson's neighborhood found out that she had become ill and had gone to the hospital. They wanted to show her how much they appreciated all she had done for them. Mrs. Johnson received many cards, gifts, and flowers while she was in the hospital. When she came home, she found her front steps covered in flowers, too. Someone had printed a large banner welcoming her home, and a balloon bouquet was tied to her mailbox. On her door was a note explaining that some of the neighbors would be bringing her dinner every day for a whole week. Mrs. Johnson felt happy to live in such a wonderful neighborhood.

Complete the Character's Motivation Worksheet for this story.

© HMH Supplemental Publishers Inc. All rights reserved.
Summarizing Strategies Grade 6, SV 9781419099908

Character's Motivation

Read the story below.

Teaching Mutt

Chas loved Mutt—the boy and the dog were the best of friends. Still, even Chas felt pestered by Mutt pretty much every day.

In the morning, Mutt yipped and yapped until Chas climbed out of bed, pulled on his robe, and let Mutt out. When he came in, Mutt yapped and yipped until Chas fed him and got him fresh water. But the pestering didn't stop there. Mutt yipped when he wanted to play. He yapped when he wanted to be petted. The yipping and yapping usually got Mutt just what he wanted.

Then one day, a trainer came to meet Mutt. "Mutt, you are a fine dog," the trainer said, scratching Mutt in his favorite spot behind his left ear. "But you need to learn some manners. You need to stop being a pest."

For a week, the trainer worked with Mutt. She taught him to wait patiently for his food. She taught him to scratch the back door gently when he needed to go out. He also learned to bring a ball when he wanted to play and roll on his back when he wanted a belly rub.

Complete the Character's Motivation Worksheet for this story.

© HMH Supplemental Publishers Inc. All rights reserved.

Summarizing Strategies Grade 6, SV 9781419099908

Name _____   Date _____

Character's Motivation Worksheet

Story Title _____

Complete the Character Motivation Table based on what you've read.

Character's name:		
	Action	**Motivation**
1.		
2.		
3.		
4.		

Summary: Use the information in the Character Motivation Table to write a summary of the reading.

_____

_____

_____

© HMH Supplemental Publishers Inc. All rights reserved.

Summarizing Strategies Grade 6, SV 9781419099908

Character Traits

Presentation and Model

Strategy: Summarizing what a story character is like

Sometimes an author does not tell you everything you need to know about a character, so you must analyze the character. When you analyze a character you use facts from the story to figure out how a character thinks or feels.

Read the story below.

"Shhh!" warned Ashley. "Don't wake her up, or you'll spoil the surprise," she reminded her younger brothers. The three children slipped downstairs and shut the kitchen door behind them. Then Ashley started assigning jobs. "Danny, get out the skillet. Jeff, you mix the pancakes. I'll get coffee going."

"Okay, okay, Ash," said Danny. "We know what to do. We're not babies!"

"I'm still a baby," said Jeff. "Mom says so."

"You act like a baby, for sure," teased Danny. "Coochie coochie coo!" he crooned as he tickled his little brother.

"Knock it off, you two, or we'll never get done," Ashley said. She knew this would have been easier if she just did it alone, but she also knew that her mom would be very happy to know that they had all worked together to make this breakfast for her on her birthday.

With as little noise as possible, the kids made breakfast. They arranged it on a tray. Then Jeff said, "Hold on—I'm going to pick a few roses from the bush outside." He brought the flowers in and placed them on the tray.

"Nice touch!" Danny said. Proudly, the three children carried breakfast up to their mom.

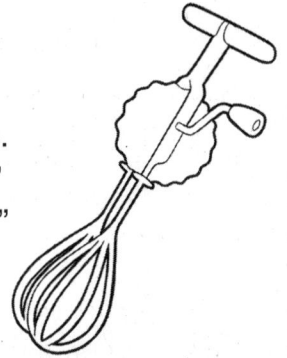

Complete the Character Profile for Ashley based on what you've read.

Character's Name
Ashley

What the Character Wants
to surprise mom, and make her happy

What the Character Thinks
Mom will be happy the kids worked together.

How the Character Feels
proud of the breakfast they made for their mom

What the Character Says
Don't wake her up, or you'll spoil the surprise.

What the Character Does
assigns jobs, makes coffee, helped make breakfast

Summary: Use the information in the Character Profile to write a summary of the story.

Ashley and her brothers sneak down and make breakfast for their mom on her birthday.

They work together and are proud of what they have done.

© HMH Supplemental Publishers Inc. All rights reserved.
Summarizing Strategies Grade 6, SV 9781419099908

Character Traits

Read the story below.

It's the Thought that Counts

Morris rushed to the ringing phone and picked it up. "Hello, Morris?" said his dad. "I'll be a little late coming home from work this evening. But don't worry—it's because I just found out that I got the promotion!"

"That's great, Dad," said Morris. "I'll see you when you get home."

As he hung up, Morris wondered how he could congratulate his father on his hard work. He decided to make a special dinner. He'd never cooked much before, but he figured he could handle it.

Morris was wrong. He made a salad by tearing up lettuce and chopping carrots, but then he dropped the bowl while putting it in the refrigerator. He had to rinse the salad off again. Then, as he was setting the table, he broke two glasses and a plate. He tried to heat up a frozen pie, but the crust burned. Then he forgot the most important ingredient in the macaroni and cheese—the cheese!

"I must be more nervous about cooking than I thought," Morris said. "Time for Plan B." Morris picked up the phone and ordered pizza.

"With any luck," he thought, "I'll have this mess cleaned up before Dad gets here."

Complete the Character Traits Worksheet for Morris and this story.

© HMH Supplemental Publishers Inc. All rights reserved.
Summarizing Strategies Grade 6, SV 9781419099908

Character Traits

Read the story below.

A Work of Art

Martin had been working on this project since he had visited the Johnson Space Center in Houston three weeks ago. The model had almost jumped off the shelf at him when he was in the gift shop. Martin loved to put together models and thought there was no better way to remember his trip than with a space shuttle in his room.

Martin was so proud of the model that he invited several of his friends over to see it. As they arrived, they all noticed that he had draped a cloth over it so he could unveil it to them at one time. "Ladies and gentlemen, I present the *Discovery!*" Martin pulled the sheet off with a beaming smile.

Everyone loved it. They couldn't believe how realistic it looked. "That's the best part about building models," Martin replied. "It's fun to put them together, but painting them and adding decals so that they look just right is the part I love. I found all kinds of pictures on the internet so that I could make it look as real as possible."

They all congratulated him on a job well done.

Complete the Character Traits Worksheet for this story.

© HMH Supplemental Publishers Inc. All rights reserved. Summarizing Strategies Grade 6, SV 9781419099908

Name _____ Date _____

Character Traits Worksheet

Story Title _____

Complete the Character Profile based on what you've read.

**What the
Character Wants**

Character's Name

_____

**What the
Character Thinks**

How the Character Feels

**What the
Character Says**

What the Character Does

Summary: Use the information in the Character Profile to write a summary of
the reading.

_____

_____

_____

© HMH Supplemental Publishers Inc. All rights reserved.
Summarizing Strategies Grade 6, SV 9781419099908

Implied Main Idea

Presentation and Model

Strategy: Identifying a main idea that is not clearly stated

Often, writers state the main idea of a piece of writing clearly. You can underline the idea, right in the text. Other times, writers use an implied main idea. *Implied* means "suggested."

Read the story below.

Tessa stepped into her room and then right back out into the hall. "Oh, my—what smells so bad in my room?" she wondered. Quickly she crossed the room and opened a window to let in the fresh spring air. "I guess it's time for some spring cleaning."

The room was indeed a mess. Tessa couldn't begin to guess what was causing the bad smell. "Well, I suppose I'll just start at the top of the mess and work down," she decided. Clothes, books, and magazines were on top—on top of everything, as far as Tessa could tell. She sorted them into the closet, drawers, laundry hamper, shelves, and recycling bin.

Then she tackled the next layer: CDs, video games, and notes from friends all found their correct places. Now Tessa could see the floor, but she still wasn't sure what smelled so bad. She followed her nose to the dresser, dropped to her knees, and peered below. There was an apple, slowly shriveling up. "Snow White would never be tempted by this," thought Tessa with disgust as she used a paper towel to reach the apple.

Complete the Implied Idea graphic based on what you've read.

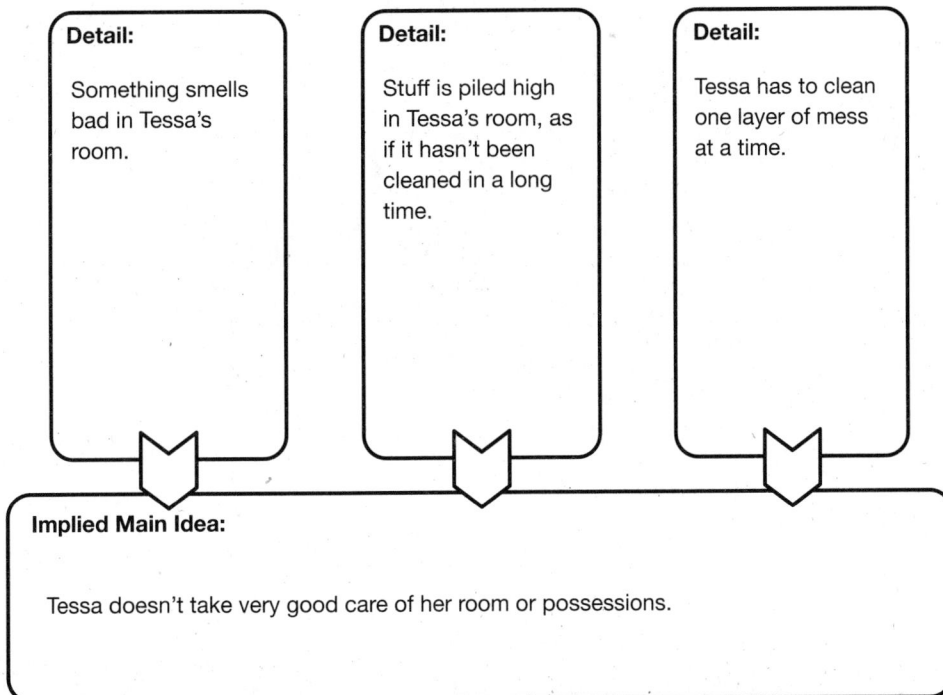

Detail:	Detail:	Detail:
Something smells bad in Tessa's room.	Stuff is piled high in Tessa's room, as if it hasn't been cleaned in a long time.	Tessa has to clean one layer of mess at a time.

Implied Main Idea:

Tessa doesn't take very good care of her room or possessions.

Summary: Use the information in the Implied Idea graphic to write a summary of the story.

Tessa does not clean her room very often. When she smells something, she finally starts cleaning it up.

© HMH Supplemental Publishers Inc. All rights reserved.

Implied Main Idea

Read the story below.

One More Time

Carol would have sighed with contentment if she hadn't been breathing so hard and concentrating on her balance. The soft swoosh of snow filled her ears, and she could smell the spicy evergreens along the slope. Faster skiers passed her, calling out "To your right!" and "To your left!" to warn her. "Could anything be better than skiing?" she thought in passing.

Carol was a good skier. Her movements were graceful and efficient, and her muscles flexed as she felt the little bumps and dips of the slopes under her skis. She never felt the cold. The wind energized her! In fact, until her parents insisted that she come in and warm up, she stayed on the slopes for "just one more run."

Complete the Implied Main Idea Worksheet for this story.

Implied Main Idea

Read the article below.

The Hippo

Have you ever seen hippos at the zoo? These enormous creatures, whether in the water or on land, look slow and sweet. But the hippo's looks are deceiving. Hippopotamus means "horse of the water," and like horses, hippos can move fast when they need to. A hippopotamus can run on the bottom of a lake or river at eight miles an hour. On land, it can run as fast as a person. And the hippo swims fast, too.

Where people and hippos share waterways, people quickly learn that hippos rule the water. If a boat comes too close to a hippo, the animal can easily tip the boat, spilling passengers and cargo into the water. In fact, many people who use the waterways where hippos live know they can be deadly, and fear them more than crocodiles.

So as you view the hippo safely from behind the fence at the zoo, keep in mind the real power of these big, cute creatures.

Complete the Implied Main Idea Worksheet for this article.

© HMH Supplemental Publishers Inc. All rights reserved.

Name _____   Date _____

Teacher's Toolbox

Implied Main Idea Worksheet

Story Title _____

Complete the Implied Idea graphic based on what you've read.

Detail:	Detail:	Detail:

Implied Main Idea:

Summary: Use the information in the Implied Idea graphic to write a summary of the reading.

_____

_____

_____

Sequence of Events

Presentation and Model

Strategy: Identifying the order of steps in a process

Sequences appear in many kinds of writing. You may see them, for example, in a news article, recipe, biography, or set of instructions. Summarizing sequences helps you follow directions, understand an event, and learn new information.

Read the story below.

Ms. Salazar's car was dirty. And no wonder! Just last weekend, she'd driven down dusty roads to visit an orchard and pick apples. After that trip, the car needed cleaning inside and out.

Ms. Salazar got out the hose and hooked it up tightly to the outside water faucet. She got some soap, a bucket, a sponge, and some old towels from the garage. After she assembled everything she needed, Ms. Salazar parked the car in the yard and went to work. First she filled the bucket with water and added soap. She turned off the water and scrubbed the car all over with the sponge. She saw that she needed a stiff brush to get into the small spots, so she found one and used it, too. Then she turned the water back on and rinsed the car thoroughly.

Ms. Salazar dried the car with towels, but she saw that the windows had streaks. She went to the recycle bin and pulled out several sheets of newspaper, which she wadded up and used to wipe the windows until they were free of streaks.

Phew! Ms. Salazar's car was clean again on the outside, but she was tired. And she still had to clean the inside!

Complete the Sequence Peacock based on what you've read.

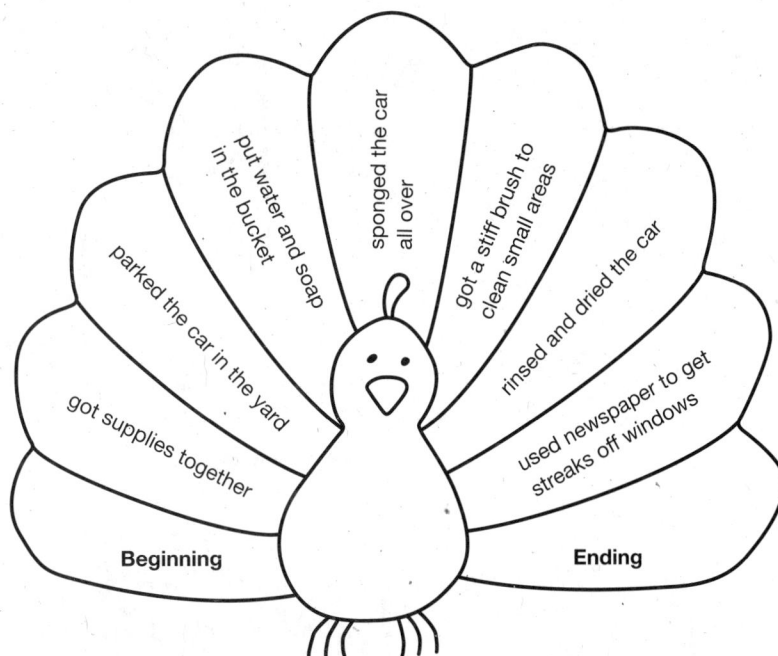

Peacock with tail feathers labeled: parked the car in the yard · put water and soap in the bucket · sponged the car all over · got a stiff brush to clean small areas · rinsed and dried the car · used newspaper to get streaks off windows · got supplies together. **Beginning** (left) — **Ending** (right)

Summary: Use the information in the Sequence Peacock to write a summary of the story.

Ms. Salazar cleaned the outside of her car by scrubbing it, rinsing it, drying it, and cleaning the windows with newspaper.

© HMH Supplemental Publishers Inc. All rights reserved.

Sequence of Events

Read the article below.

How the Body Uses Fat

Although some people think that you shouldn't eat fatty foods, they are wrong! Your body uses fat in many ways. Fat covers important body organs. If you get hurt, a layer of fat can protect those organs. Fat also acts as insulation by keeping body heat in. Fat can keep you alive. If you were without food for a very long time, your body would burn stored fat for energy. In addition, your body uses small amounts of fat to repair cells.

Here's the process by which the body uses fat, step by step: First, you eat food. As the food is digested, fat in the food enters the bloodstream and moves to fat cells throughout the body. The fat is stored in these cells until the body needs energy. When energy is needed, fat reenters the bloodstream and travels to the body parts that need energy. Oxygen from the air you breathe mixes with the fat to burn it. Then, the fat releases energy into the muscle cells, which helps you throw a ball, ride a bike, or do any other activity.

Complete the Sequence of Events Worksheet for this article.

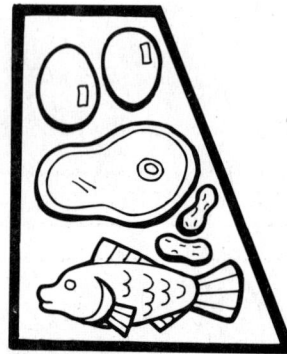

Sequence of Events

Read the story below.

The New Tank

Sergio had told Ellen about the Air-Alive Fish Tank he had bought the previous month. His fish really seemed more active and happy. After all Sergio had said, Ellen decided to get one for her fish. Her main concern was how hard the tank would be to set up.

"First, you should unpack all the parts and match them to the parts list," Sergio said. "After that, gently rinse each part so that dust does not get into the air tubes. Then you'll need to use the air tube diagram to hook the air tubes to each other and to the air stone and filter. It sounds harder than it is," he added with a smile.

"Next, you lay the air tubes and air stone on the bottom of the tank, and cover them with aquarium gravel," he continued. "If you want to have plants in your tank, stick them in the gravel, and then slowly add water to the tank."

"That doesn't sound too hard," Ellen admitted. "I've heard about some that take forever to set up."

"Don't forget to add four drops of the Tank-Clear solution, and then wait for the water to clear before you add your fish."

Complete the Sequence of Events Worksheet for this story.

© HMH Supplemental Publishers Inc. All rights reserved.
Summarizing Strategies Grade 6, SV 9781419099908

Teacher's
Toolbox

Sequence of Events Worksheet

Story Title _____

Complete the Sequence Peacock based on what you've read.

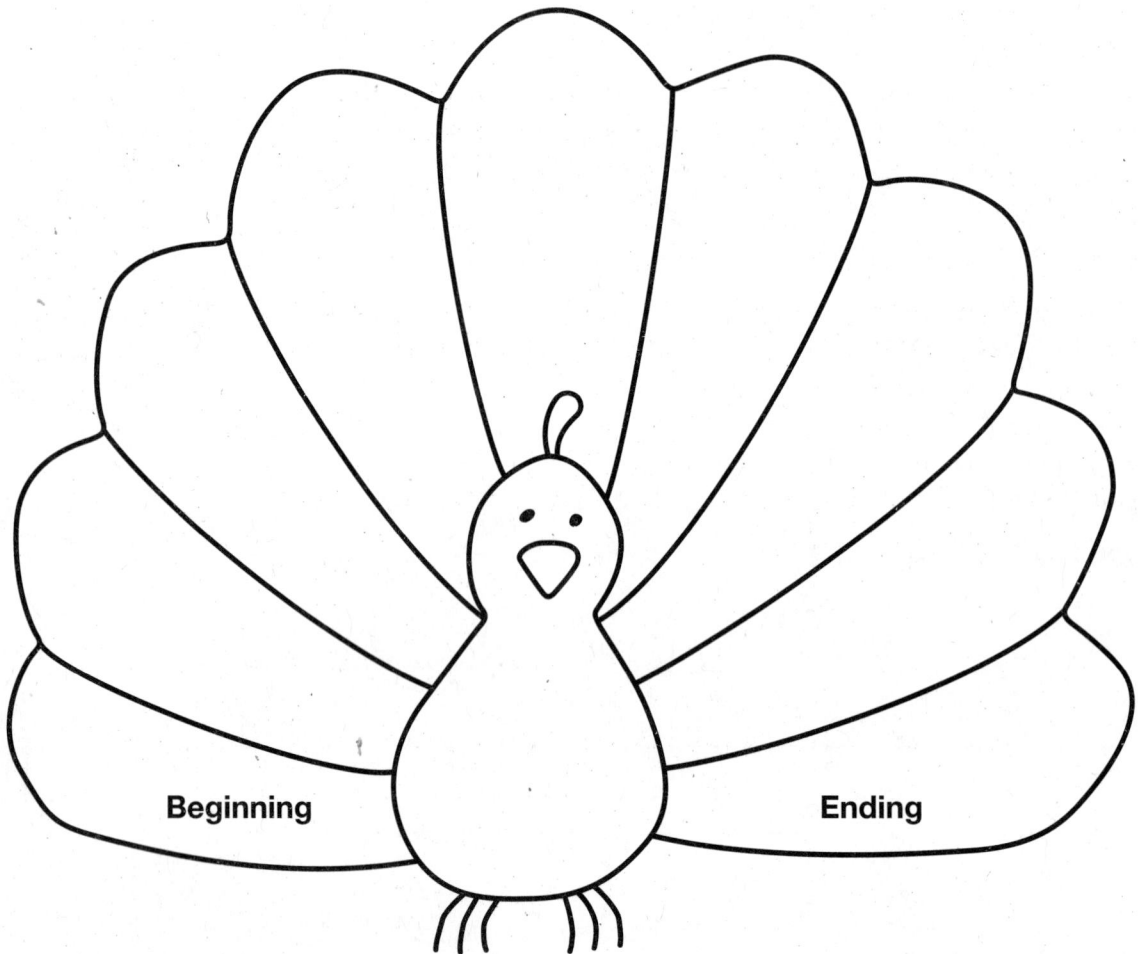

Beginning   **Ending**

Summary: Use the information in the Sequence Peacock to write a summary of
the reading.

_____

_____

_____

Fact and Opinion

Presentation and Model

Strategy: Distinguishing between facts and opinions in what you read

A fact is a piece of information that can be proven or confirmed. For example, a word's meaning is a fact. You can check it in a dictionary. The height of a mountain is a fact. You can confirm it by looking in an atlas.

An opinion is what someone thinks or believes based on facts. The same fact can lead to different opinions. Think about the height of a mountain again. One person might say a 7,000-foot mountain is "really tall." Another person might say, "No, 14,000 feet is tall—this mountain is small." The two people have formed different opinions based on the same fact.

Read the story below.

The wind blew across the lake, creating mysterious swirls on the surface of the water. The last of the leaves were lifted from the trees and danced over the water in a frenzy. Overhead, ducks and geese flew south, heading for warmer climates.

Jenny loved this time of the year. The temperatures were cooler, but she could still get by with a sweater. It would be several weeks before she had to take the bulky, annoying coat out of the closet. In the meantime, she would enjoy the lovely colors and textures of the season. This was truly the best time of year.

Complete the Fact Fingers based on what you've read.

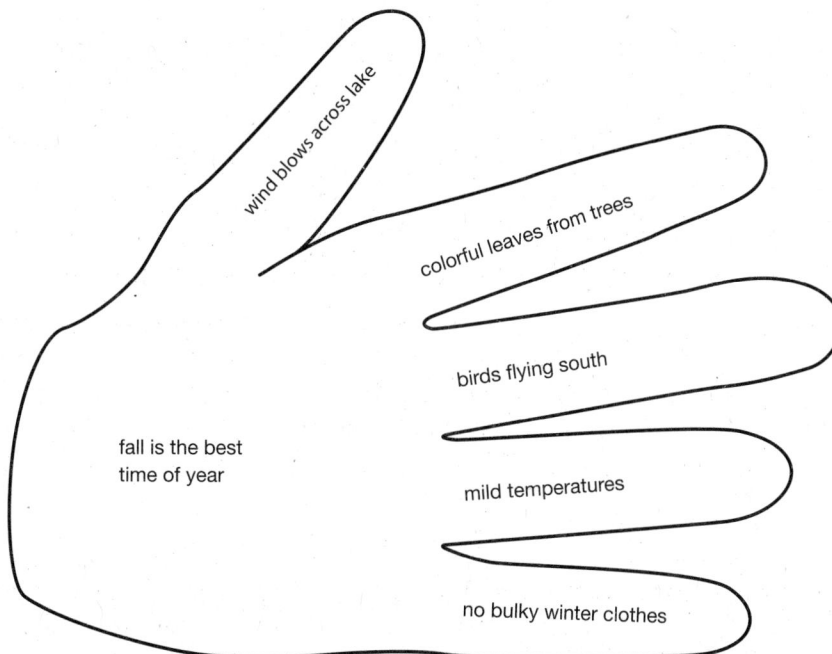

wind blows across lake

colorful leaves from trees

birds flying south

fall is the best time of year

mild temperatures

no bulky winter clothes

Summary: Use the information in the Fact Fingers to write a summary of the story.

Jenny wears a sweater by the lake on a cool, windy fall day. She sees leaves falling and geese flying south.

© HMH Supplemental Publishers Inc. All rights reserved.

Fact and Opinion

Read the article below.

Sheep Around the World

Sheep and shepherds may seem like images out of nursery rhymes and fairy tales. Bo-Peep and her lost sheep and the shepherd boy that cried "Wolf!" may come to mind. But sheep are an important livestock animal throughout the world, providing shepherds— the people who herd and care for the sheep—with income, wool, and food.

Some breeds of sheep raised in the United States are the Merino, the Hampshire, and the Cheviot. Some people think that Merino wool is the best of all wools. While all sheep are cute, the Karakul, also called fat-tail sheep, are found in Asia and are the cutest. Wild sheep, too, are found in Asia, northern Africa, and southern Europe. The bighorn, found in the Rocky Mountains, is another wild breed. Its ability to leap gracefully up a stony mountainside is marvelous.

Complete the Fact and Opinion Worksheet for this article.

© HMH Supplemental Publishers Inc. All rights reserved.

Fact and Opinion

Read the article below.

A Slithery Friend

It's a fact that snakes make the best pets! Most people are uncomfortable even thinking about snakes, but there are several good reasons to want a snake for a pet. First, snakes are very quiet. They will not wake up the neighbors by barking at night or keep anyone in the house awake. This makes them the perfect pet for apartment-dwellers.

Second, snakes are not destructive. They do not chew shoes, shred curtains, or dig holes under the fence. Surely everyone would like such a peaceful pet!

Also, since snakes are confined to a cage, they are easy to care for. And believe it or not, snakes have personalities and can be very affectionate! They are interesting to watch, and many are very beautifully colored.

Finally, with the right kind of snake and a well-placed warning sign, the chances of a burglar entering your home will be greatly reduced!

Complete the Fact and Opinion Worksheet for this article.

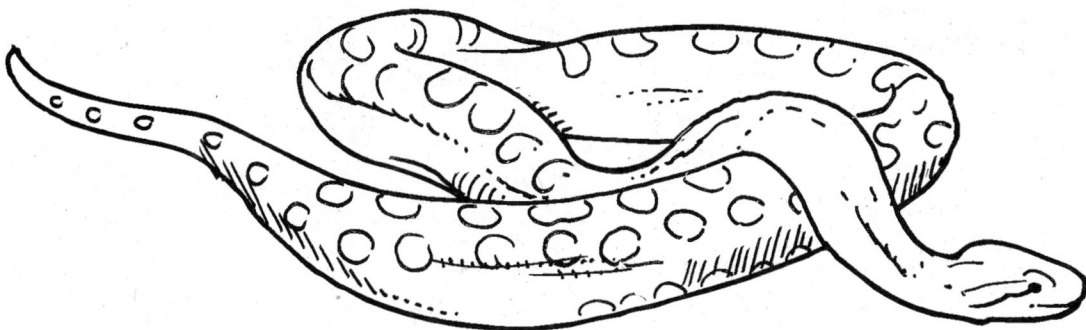

Name _____ Date _____

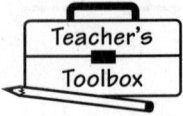

Fact and Opinion Worksheet

Story Title _____

Complete the Fact Fingers based on what you've read.

Summary: Use the information in the Fact Fingers to write a summary of the reading.

_____

_____

_____

Making Predictions

Presentation and Model

Strategy: Predicting what will happen next in what you are reading

When you read a story, you keep track of the events that have already happened. You can also think ahead—you can make predictions about what will happen next. Making predictions keeps you engaged with the story and helps you understand the plot.

Read the story below.

Bonita sat with her mother in the eye doctor's office. She was nervous because she'd never been to an eye doctor before. Bonita's mother sat next to her. She was worried because Bonita's schoolwork had not been as good as it usually was. Bonita seemed to try very hard, but she often made mistakes at school. Bonita had also been complaining that her eyes were feeling tired and that she was having headaches. Her teacher suggested that Bonita have her eyes examined because sometimes poor eyesight could cause these kinds of problems.

The nurse called Bonita's name. The tests took a little over an hour. After the tests, the doctor told Bonita that she needed glasses. Bonita didn't want to wear glasses. Bonita's mother let her pick frames she liked best, but she knew how hard it would be for Bonita to adjust to wearing glasses.

Complete the Prediction Chart based on what you've read.

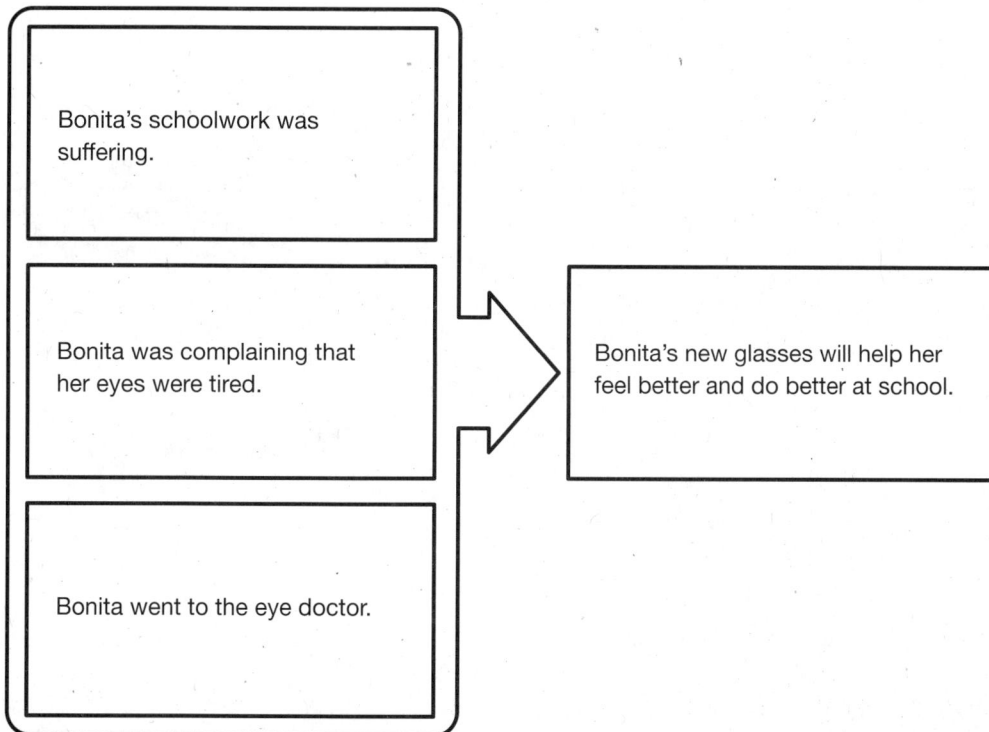

Bonita's schoolwork was suffering.
Bonita was complaining that her eyes were tired.
Bonita went to the eye doctor.

→ Bonita's new glasses will help her feel better and do better at school.

Summary: Use the information in the Prediction Chart to write a summary of the story.

Bonita was having trouble in school and her eyes were bothering her. Bonita's mom took her to see the eye doctor. After the testing, Bonita picked out the glasses she wanted.

Making Predictions

Read the story below.

Playing Solo

Dana was sitting by herself at the side of the stage in the huge auditorium. She held her violin in her clammy hands as she went through her music in her head. In the background she could hear the boy performing on the stage. He seemed to play as if no one were listening—no parents, no crowd of young musicians, and especially no judges. Why couldn't she be so calm? For as long as she had played, going out on stage alone had never been easy for her. She shifted her violin to her lap and wiped her sweaty hands on her dress.

The boy finished his piece and bowed gracefully to the judges. The audience broke into appreciative applause. Then Dana's name was announced over the speaker. She took a deep breath. What if she fainted from nervousness before she even got to the stage? Hands shaking, knees wobbly, she climbed the stairs to the stage and bowed to the judges.

Complete the Making Predictions Worksheet for this story.

© HMH Supplemental Publishers Inc. All rights reserved.
Making Predictions
Summarizing Strategies Grade 6, SV 9781419099908

Making Predictions

Read the story below.

Gone Fishing

"I'll never catch a fish," whined Aidan. "We've been sitting here for hours! I'm tired. Let's go home."

"You're right," Uncle Whit answered. "You'll never catch a fish if you go home now. We've only been here one hour, so let's keep at it for a while longer."

"Stupid fish—they don't like my bait. I'm hungry. Let's go home," Aidan begged again.

Uncle Whit laughed. "You know what they call fishing, don't you? Drowning worms— and that's what we're doing. But trust me. Once you catch your first fish, you won't want to quit and go home. Look—there's a tug on your line now! Reel in slowly!" He helped Aidan pull the line in. "Oops, that one got away."

Now Aidan was really discouraged. He looked at his empty hook in disgust. "Let's go home," he repeated.

Complete the Making Predictions Worksheet for this story.

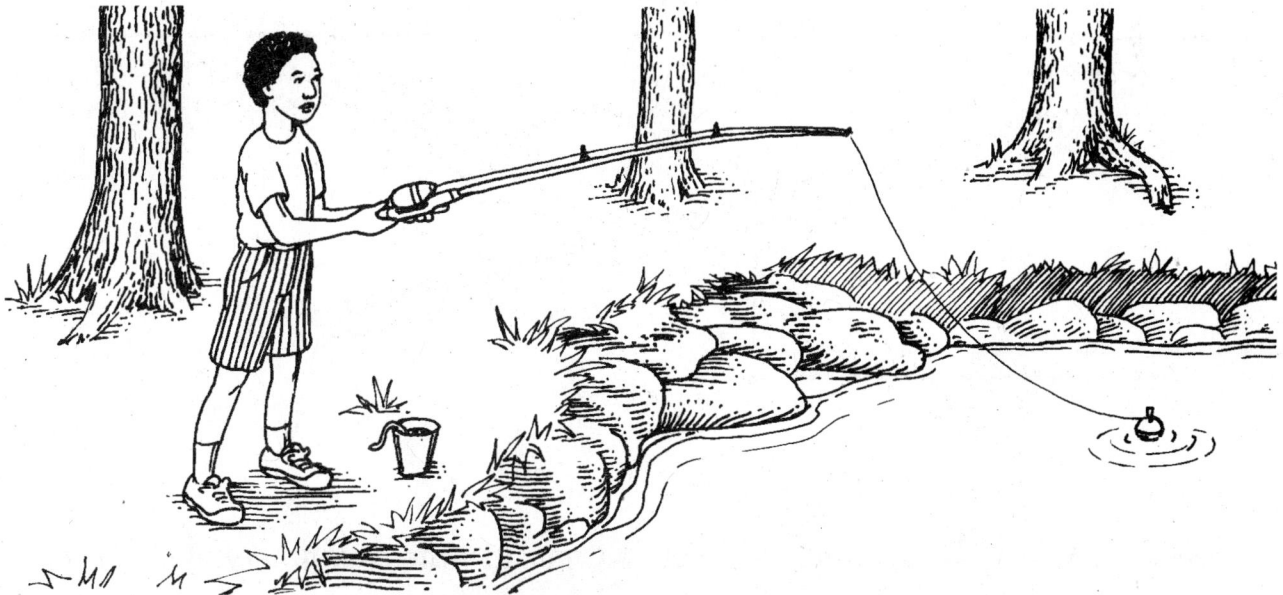

Name _____   Date _____

Teacher's Toolbox

Making Predictions Worksheet

Story Title _____

Complete the Prediction Chart based on what you've read.

Summary: Use the information in the Prediction Chart to write a summary of the reading.

_____

_____

_____

© HMH Supplemental Publishers Inc. All rights reserved.
Making Predictions
Summarizing Strategies Grade 6, SV 9781419099908

Cause and Effect

Presentation and Model

Strategy: Identifying a cause and its effect in what you read

A cause is an event than makes another event happen. The effect is the next event that happens as a result of the cause. You see causes and effects around you every day:

Cause: You eat lunch. ⟶ **Effect:** You are no longer hungry.

Cause: You forget your jacket. ⟶ **Effect:** You get cold walking to school.

Read the story below.

Emma's house was in an uproar. She and her parents had been planning this night for over two weeks. Emma had handwritten all the invitations, Mrs. Davis had ordered the perfect cake, and Mr. Davis had set up a karaoke machine for the kids.

Now that the big day was finally here, everyone was extra busy! Mrs. Davis had shopped all afternoon and was putting her purchases away. Mr. Davis had cleaned the apartment and put up decorations while Emma was at school. Now, Mrs. Davis and Emma were preparing food and getting ready to welcome all the guests. Emma's birthday was a big event—and what a big mess there would be to clear up the next day!

Complete the Cause and Effect Meltdown based on what you've read.

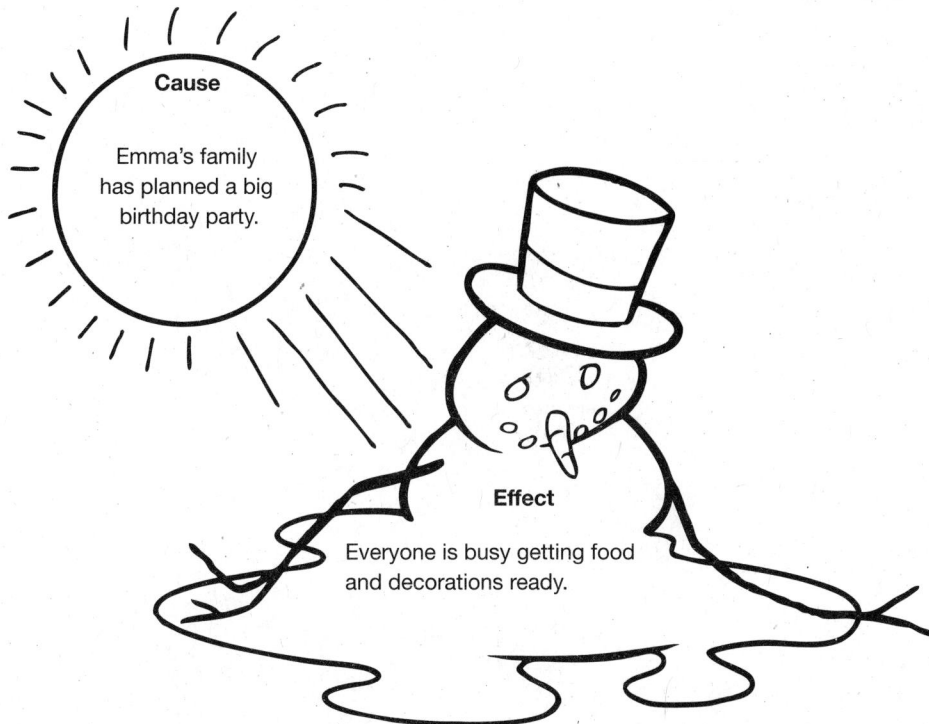

Cause

Emma's family has planned a big birthday party.

Effect

Everyone is busy getting food and decorations ready.

Summary: Use the information in the Cause and Effect Meltdown to write a summary of the story.

Emma's upcoming birthday party causes her family to be busy with preparations.

© HMH Supplemental Publishers Inc. All rights reserved.

Cause and Effect

Read the story below.

Picture Perfect

Stefan had worked very hard on his exhibit for the fair. He planned to enter the photography contest. Over the summer, he took more than two hundred pictures. Some of the pictures had people in them, others had animals, and some were just scenery. Stefan also took some pictures in black and white, while others were in color. It was hard to choose just forty photographs for his scrapbook. He made sure to try to include a variety of different styles, but the largest section of his scrapbook was devoted to close-ups of wildflowers. He decided the judges would like them because of all the bright, vivid colors.

After picking out the pictures he wanted to include, he laid them out two per page. He spent hours carefully arranging and pasting them onto the pages. Stefan also took the time to write a brief description of each photograph and placed it by its picture. It told where and when the picture was taken, as well as listed the camera settings he had used. When Stefan walked in the house with the first place trophy, it was no surprise to his parents. Everyone knew that all his hard work would pay off.

Complete the Cause and Effect Worksheet for this story.

© HMH Supplemental Publishers Inc. All rights reserved.

Summarizing Strategies Grade 6, SV 9781419099908

Cause and Effect

Read the article below.

I See the Moon

Since you were a little child, you've watched the moon. Maybe "moon" was one of your first words. The bright, beautiful moon is a favorite sky object of many people, young and old. But do you know why the moon appears to change size and shape?

On some nights the moon is just a pale sliver against the dark blue sky. On others, the full moon reflects so much light that you can almost read by it. And sometimes you can see a half moon in the daytime sky. It seems that you can almost see right through it.

What causes these changes, which are called the phases of the moon? One cause accounts for all of these views of the moon: the position of the sun, Earth, and moon.

The moon, of course, does not really shine. It produces no light of its own. Rather, it reflects the sun's light. How much of that reflected light we see on Earth depends on where the moon is located in orbit around our planet. When the moon is located between the Earth and the sun, more of the reflected light is hidden from our view, so the moon looks like a sliver. When the moon is located behind the Earth, more of the reflected light is visible, so the moon looks full. These different shapes of reflected light are referred to as the phases of the moon.

Complete the Cause and Effect Worksheet for this article.

© HMH Supplemental Publishers Inc. All rights reserved.
Summarizing Strategies Grade 6, SV 9781419099908

Name _____   Date _____

Cause and Effect Worksheet

Teacher's Toolbox

Story Title _____

Complete the Cause and Effect Meltdown based on what you've read.

Cause

Effect

Summary: Use the information in the Cause and Effect Meltdown to write a summary of the reading.

_____

_____

_____

Cause and Multiple Effects

Presentation and Model

Strategy: Summarizing causal relationships that involve more than one cause or effect

Causal relationships are the connections between events that happen. Sometimes a single cause leads to a single effect. Sometimes, however, a single cause may have many effects. You must read carefully to identify each part of the causal relationship.

Read the article below.

Why should students get plenty of sleep? This is a question that many young people ask. After all, it's more fun to stay up watching movies, listening to music, or reading a good book. But students don't realize just how much their bodies need sleep. Getting enough sleep can help the body in many ways. First, the proper rest helps the body stay strong enough to fight off germs and infections. Second, a good night of sleep helps the body use food efficiently. Finally, getting the right amount of sleep gives the brain a chance to rest so that you can think clearly the next day. So the next time you're considering staying up too late, do your body a favor and get some sleep!

Complete the Cause with Multiple Effects Diagram based on what you've read.

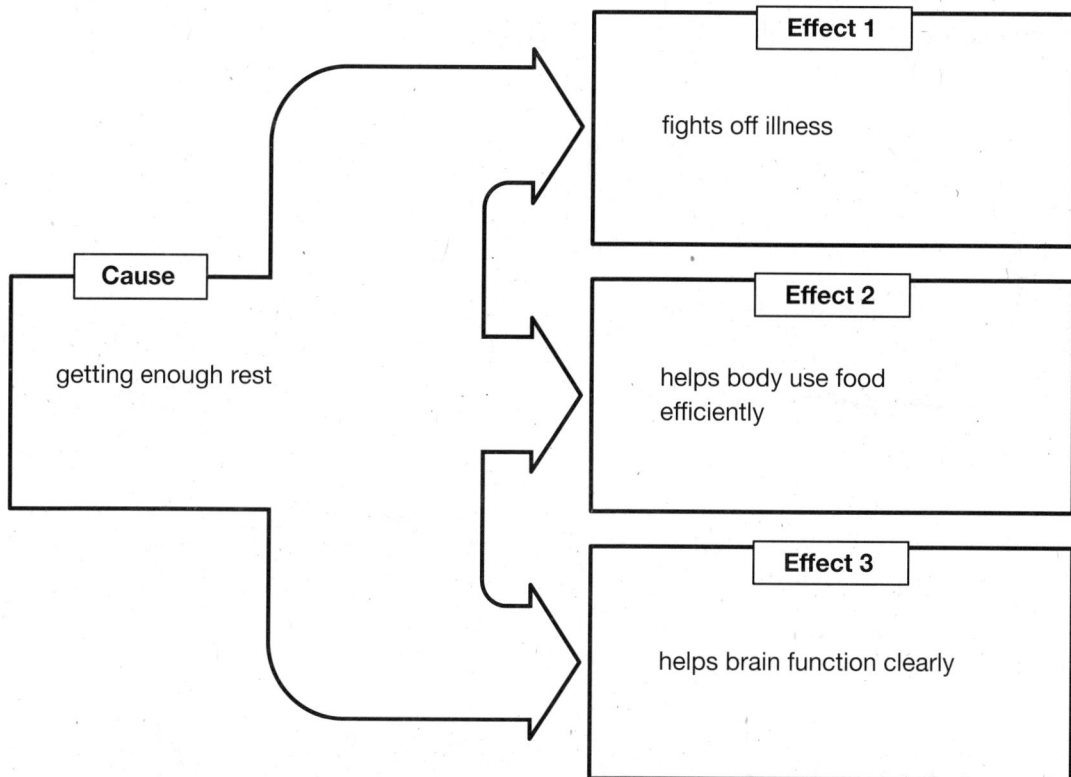

Cause		Effect 1
getting enough rest	→	fights off illness
	→	**Effect 2**
		helps body use food efficiently
	→	**Effect 3**
		helps brain function clearly

Summary: Use the information in the Cause with Multiple Effects Diagram to write a summary of the article.

Getting enough sleep is very important for the body. It helps fight illness, aids in using food efficiently, and provides a clear mind.

© HMH Supplemental Publishers Inc. All rights reserved.

Summarizing Strategies Grade 6, SV 9781419099908

Cause and Multiple Effects

Read the story below.

Wayne Needs a Plan

Poor Wayne! He had a tough time with school. One thing after another seemed to go wrong. He never seemed to get his homework right. It wasn't that he answered the questions wrong; he answered the wrong questions. If he had a big project due, he would get it done, but then forget to turn it in on the right day. As for after-school activities, forget it! He could never keep the times straight.

Yet Wayne was a smart student, and his teacher knew it. One day, she gave him a little gift. It was a day planner. Then she showed him how to use it to keep track of homework, practices, and other events. For a week, she helped Wayne record important information every day before he went home so that he could remember what to turn in the next day.

The day planner has changed Wayne's life. Because of this useful tool, he rarely forgets his assignments, and he makes all his soccer practices on time. His grades have gone up, and he plans to mow lawns on weekends to make some money. He's very glad that his teacher gave him the planner.

Complete the Cause and Multiple Effects Worksheet for this story.

© HMH Supplemental Publishers Inc. All rights reserved.

Cause and Multiple Effects

Read the article below.

Trash to Treasure

Pearls are beautiful. These little globes come in various colors, from white to grey to green, and may be quite round or rather lumpy. Unlike gemstones such as diamonds and sapphires, pearls are formed by a biological process.

Pearls form inside of oysters. An oyster is a bivalve—a shell made of two halves. The shell opens so that the oyster can eat, but sometimes things that the oyster cannot eat float in. These little bits of matter irritate the soft insides of the oyster. Think of what it feels like to get a splinter in your finger. Even a tiny splinter can hurt.

The oyster defends itself against the painful bit of material by coating it in nacre. Nacre is the shiny lining inside an oyster. The oyster is already making nacre for its growing shell, so it simply applies some to the unwanted object. Over time, more and more coats of nacre cover the bit of matter. Gradually, it becomes a pearl.

Complete the Cause and Multiple Effects Worksheet for this article.

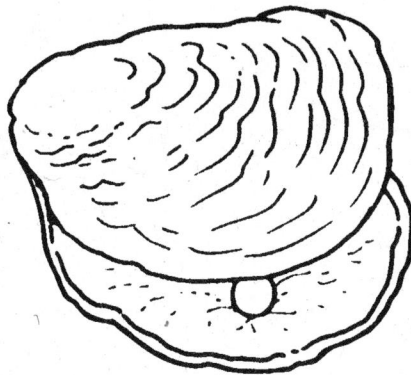

© HMH Supplemental Publishers Inc. All rights reserved.
Summarizing Strategies Grade 6, SV 9781419099908

Cause and Multiple Effects Worksheet

Teacher's Toolbox

Story Title _____

Complete the Cause with Multiple Effects Diagram based on what you've read.

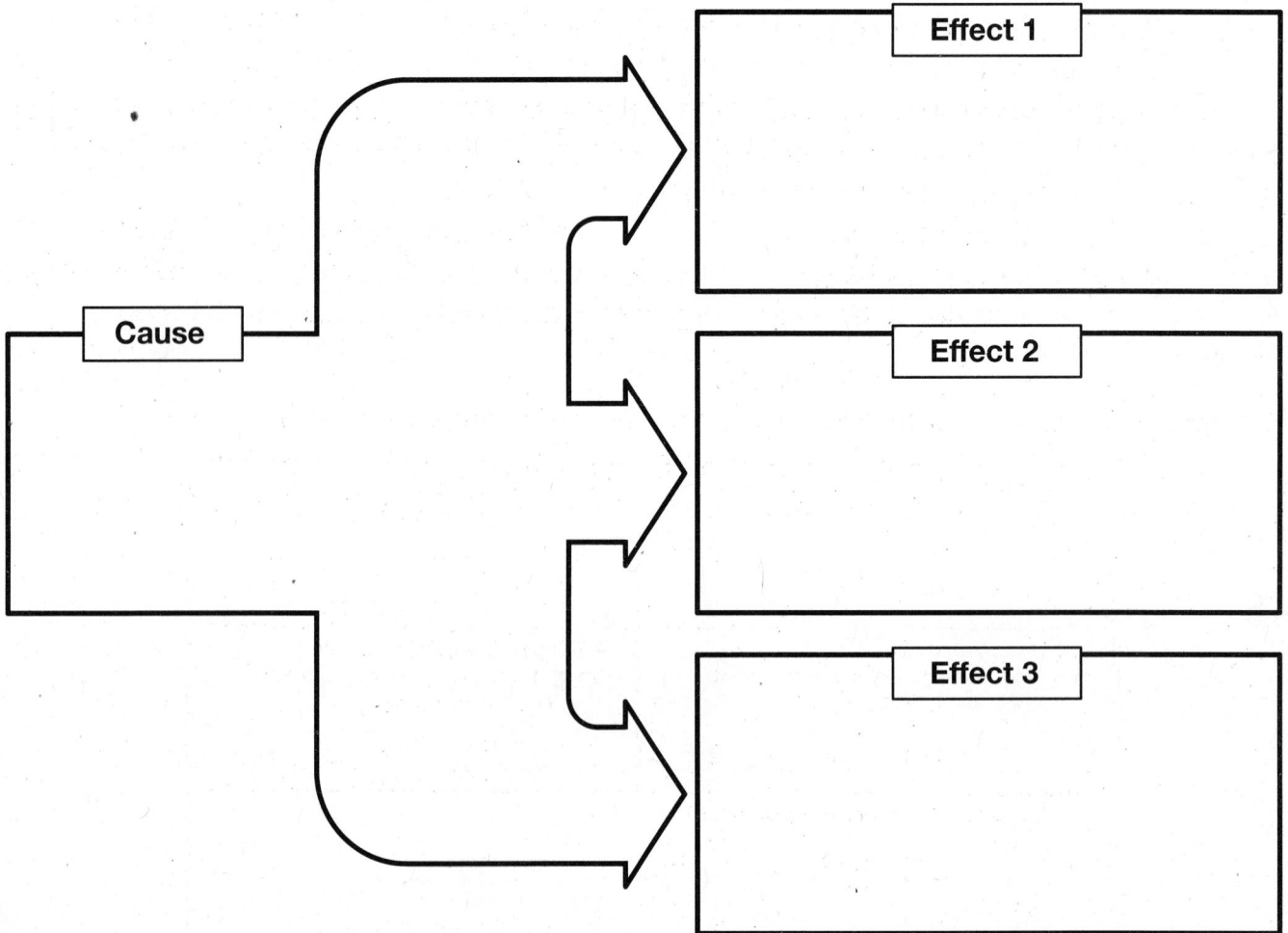

| Cause |

| Effect 1 |

| Effect 2 |

| Effect 3 |

Summary: Use the information in the Cause with Multiple Effects Diagram to write a summary of the reading.

_____

_____

_____

Author's Purpose

Presentation and Model

Strategy: Identifying the author's purpose

Authors have different reasons for writing stories. Sometimes an author wants to entertain a reader with a story. Other times an author may want to give the reader information about a subject. The reason is also known as the purpose, and sometimes stories have more than one.

Read the article below.

Penguins are very well suited to live in the cold climates of the world. They have waterproof feathers and thick layers of fat to help keep them warm. Some male penguins actually have extra rolls of fat, which they use to keep their newborn penguins warm.

Long, long ago, penguins were capable of flying as most other birds do. But over time, their wings developed into flippers that now function as paddles. They glide through the cold water, using their flippers and webbed feet, looking for small fish to eat.

Perhaps the most interesting thing of all about a penguin is the way it walks. Penguins actually waddle because they have such short legs. But penguins are also expert belly-surfers. They can slide on their stomachs, again using their flippers and feet to push themselves forward.

Complete the Author's Purpose Table based on what you've read.

To Inform Did I learn something as I read? ___✓___ Yes _____ No	To Entertain Did I smile or laugh as I read? ___✓___ Yes _____ No
To Persuade Me to Think Did the reading ask me to change what I think about something? _____ Yes ___✓___ No	To Persuade Me to Act Did the reading ask me to do something or change my behavior? _____ Yes ___✓___ No
What was the author's main purpose? to give information	
What was the author's secondary purpose, if any? to entertain	

Summary: Use the information in the Author's Purpose Table to write a summary of the article.

Penguins are birds that used to be able to fly, but no longer can. They are well suited for the cold. While they glide under water, they can be funny waddling and sliding on land.

© HMH Supplemental Publishers Inc. All rights reserved.

Author's Purpose

Read the flyer below.

Calling All Neighborhood Parents!
Important Meeting: Thursday, 7 P.M.
In the School Gym

Parents, are you worried that our children don't get enough healthy play time?

Are you concerned that our children have to play ball in the neighborhood streets?

Would you like to have a close, safe place for our children to play sports?

If so, then come to the first meeting of the New Playground Interest Group! NPIG is a group of concerned parents who want the best for their children. We intend to work with the city to plan and build a playground in our neighborhood.

Come meet your city council representative. Help us as we develop a playground and park for our children!

Complete the Author's Purpose Worksheet for this flyer.

© HMH Supplemental Publishers Inc. All rights reserved.
Summarizing Strategies Grade 6, SV 9781419099908

Author's Purpose

Read the story below.

We All Need Vacations

Jump forward in your imaginations to the year 2030! In this time, people have invented machines and robots to do all the work, from building hovercars to walking dogs. No one has a job anymore! Working is so old fashioned. You have all the time in the world to play, read, and think.

But all play and no work can be a bore, don't you think? So guess what people do in this time for vacation? They get a job! Just think: two weeks of work, all expenses paid, is the dream vacation for people in 2030. Travel agents arrange for all kinds of work vacations. Would you like to cook at a restaurant, build houses, or sell groceries? Maybe you would prefer to sit at a big, shiny table and make executive decisions? Perhaps you'd even like to dig a garden or paint a house. That can be arranged, too!

After all, playing all the time is tiring. I bet you're looking forward to a work vacation right now!

Complete the Author's Purpose Worksheet for this story.

© HMH Supplemental Publishers Inc. All rights reserved.

Name _____ Date _____

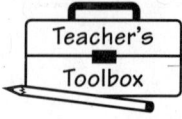

Author's Purpose Worksheet

Teacher's Toolbox

Story Title _____

Complete the Author's Purpose Table based on what you've read.

To Inform Did I learn something as I read? _____ Yes _____ No	**To Entertain** Did I smile or laugh as I read? _____ Yes _____ No
To Persuade Me to Think Did the reading ask me to change what I think about something? _____ Yes _____ No	**To Persuade Me to Act** Did the reading ask me to do something or change my behavior? _____ Yes _____ No

What was the author's main purpose?

What was the author's secondary purpose, if any?

Summary: Use the information in the Author's Purpose Table to write a summary of the reading.

_____

_____

_____

www.harcourtschoolsupply.com
© HMH Supplemental Publishers Inc. All rights reserved.

Drawing Conclusions

Presentation and Model

Strategy: Drawing conclusions from what you read

When you draw conclusions, you make a judgment based on information you read and what you already know. However, you don't want to "jump to conclusions," or draw a conclusion that is not supported by what you read. Instead, look for clear information in the reading, which leads to the judgment you make.

Read the article below.

The Sahara is the largest non-polar desert in the world. Its name actually means "desert," and it lives up to that name. This vast place, almost as large as the continental United States, is very hot and very dry. Temperatures as high as 136 degrees Fahrenheit have been recorded in the Sahara, even in the shade!

Little rain falls on this desert, but some grass does grow after rainfalls. This grass makes possible the life of herders, called nomads, who move their animals from place to place in search of grass and water. The only parts of the Sahara fit for growing crops are the oases, such as the one near the Nile River. These rare green places in the desert are usually quite small.

Complete the Conclusion Train based on what you've read.

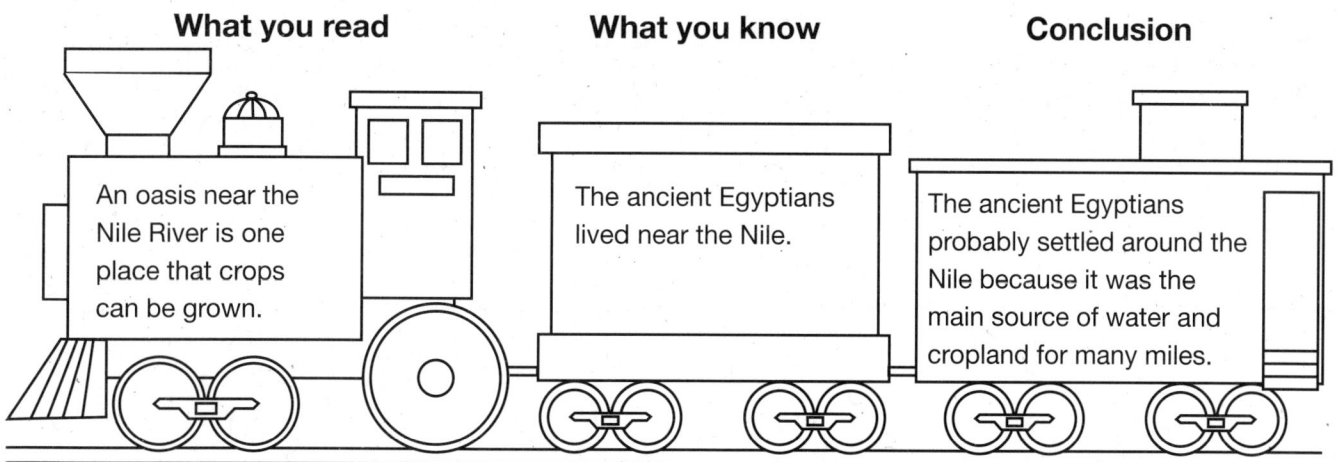

What you read	What you know	Conclusion
An oasis near the Nile River is one place that crops can be grown.	The ancient Egyptians lived near the Nile.	The ancient Egyptians probably settled around the Nile because it was the main source of water and cropland for many miles.

Summary: Use the information in the Conclusion Train to write a summary of the article.

The Sahara is the world's largest hot desert. The oasis around the Nile River is one place in

the Sahara where crops will grow.

© HMH Supplemental Publishers Inc. All rights reserved.
Summarizing Strategies Grade 6, SV 9781419099908

Drawing Conclusions

Read the story below.

The Hard Truth

Mrs. Pollard drove up to the house. She saw her son Mike sitting on the front porch. His head was down. A bat was in his hand, and his mitt lay next to him on the porch. However, Mike's baseball was nowhere to be seen.

As Mrs. Pollard walked up the steps to the porch, she noticed bits of glass by Mike's feet. Before she could say anything, Mike said, "Mom, i'm really sorry. You've told me a hundred times not to play ball in the front yard, but I did it anyway. I promise to do extra chores to pay for the repair to the window."

Mrs. Pollard took a deep breath to calm down. "Thank you for being honest and for apologizing," she said. "That makes me proud of you. I'll think of some chores for you to do to earn the repair money. You'd better start by cleaning up all this glass!"

Complete the Drawing Conclusions Worksheet for this story.

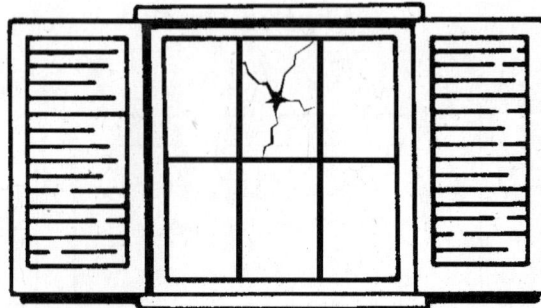

© HMH Supplemental Publishers Inc. All rights reserved.
Summarizing Strategies Grade 6, SV 9781419099908

Drawing Conclusions

Read the story below.

A Cold Wind Blows

The wind whipped around Marcia as she walked to the library. She pulled her scarf tighter around her face, but the chilly gusts still managed to filter through its soft fabric. Marcia's toes felt numb despite her wool socks and warm boots, and her fingers, curled inside her gloves, were stiff and cold.

The wind gusted more strongly, ferociously pushing Marcia back as she ducked her head and walked on. The library was only a few more blocks away; she knew that it would be nice and warm inside. She could buy a cup of hot chocolate in the library café and drink it before heading home. Marcia shivered. She did not like the idea of facing the cold wind again. Perhaps she'd call her big brother and ask him to drive over and pick her up.

Complete the Drawing Conclusions Worksheet for this story.

© HMH Supplemental Publishers Inc. All rights reserved.

Name _____   Date _____

Drawing Conclusions Worksheet

Story Title _____

Complete the Conclusion Train based on what you've read.

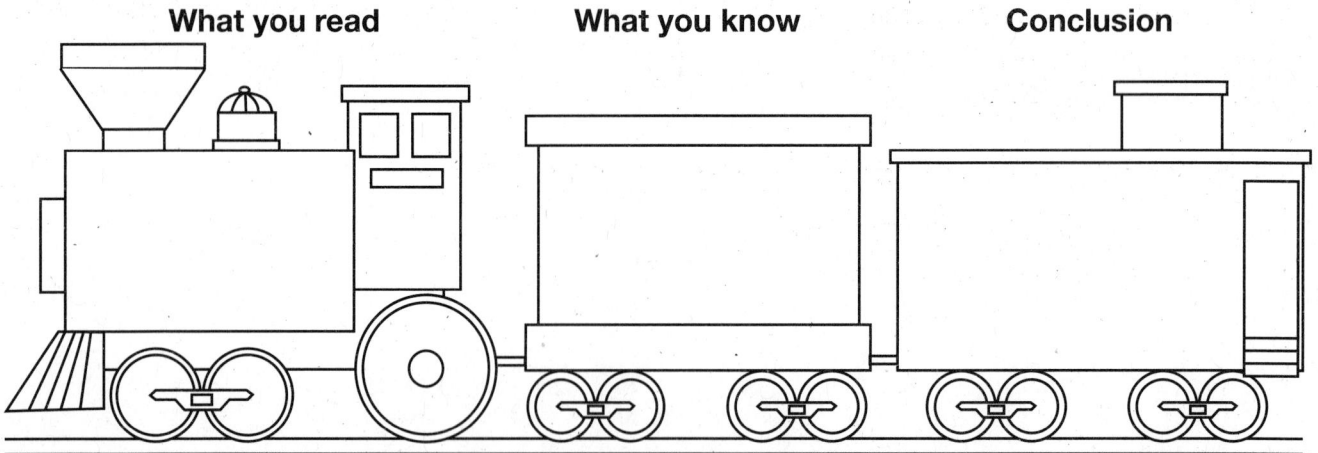

What you read　　　　**What you know**　　　　**Conclusion**

Summary: Use the information in the Conclusion Train to write a summary of the reading.

_____

_____

_____

© HMH Supplemental Publishers Inc. All rights reserved.

Making Inferences

Presentation and Model

Strategy: Making inferences based on what you read

Authors usually do not explain every idea in detail. Instead, they provide enough information to help readers make inferences, or logical guesses. You put the clues together to understand where they lead, just like solving a mystery.

Read the story below.

Will's grandfather lives on a farm. He grew up on a farm, and farming is a way of life for him. Every morning, Will's grandfather wakes up early. He has rarely slept late in his life! While he brews coffee, he feeds the cat some tuna fish in a bowl.

After a quick cup of coffee to warm him up, Grandpa walks to the barn to give the horses some oats and hay. He also takes hay to the cows in the field. The pigs are next on the feeding list; they get a special kind of pellet food. Once in a while, Grandpa takes crusts of bread to feed the fish in the pond, too.

On a farm, the animals come first. Grandpa doesn't eat until all the animals have had their food. Then he sits down to a big breakfast of fresh eggs and pancakes. This time, Will's grandmother does the feeding!

Complete the Following Footprints based on what you've read.

Clue 1: days start early

Clue 3: feed animals before eating breakfast

Clue 2: rarely ever gets a day off

Inference: farmers must be responsible and hardworking

Summary: Use the information in the Following Footprints to write a summary of the story.

Grandpa's day starts early every day. After a cup of coffee, he begins feeding all of the farm animals. Only after all the animals are fed does he get to eat breakfast himself.

© HMH Supplemental Publishers Inc. All rights reserved.

Making Inferences

Read the article below.

The Importance of Trees

In recent decades, Americans have used trees wastefully. Trees serve many functions in the world. Their roots hold nutrient-rich soil and water in place. Rain that falls in sudden storms over forests doesn't drain away because it is trapped and held beneath the trees' roots. Roots also keep the soil on riverbanks and lakes from washing away. Trees enrich the soil as well. As leaves fall to the ground and decay, they act as fertilizer to the soil, enabling new plants to take root and grow.

Trees also provide fresh air. They use carbon dioxide to convert sunlight into food. As the carbon dioxide is used, it is converted to oxygen and released into the air for people and animals to breathe.

Trees make life more comfortable, too, by creating shade, breaking storm winds, and sheltering animals. And if all these benefits are not enough, trees are also beautiful to see.

Complete the Making Inferences Worksheet for this article.

Making Inferences

Read the story below.

Step Into My Parlor

Spanning a fork in the tree's branches, a spider's web glistened in the dawn. The spider had constructed the web using her inborn talents. The work had taken her all night, but she was not tired. As the sun rose, morning dewdrops shone like crystals on the web, but the spider didn't take pride in her delicate creation. She was a hunter, and a hungry one. Perhaps she would catch something in her pretty trap today, perhaps not.

The spider was not worried. She could go for days without food; but when she did catch her prey, she would act quickly, paralyzing it with her poison and eating. Then she would repair her web or build a new one.

Complete the Making Inferences Worksheet for this story.

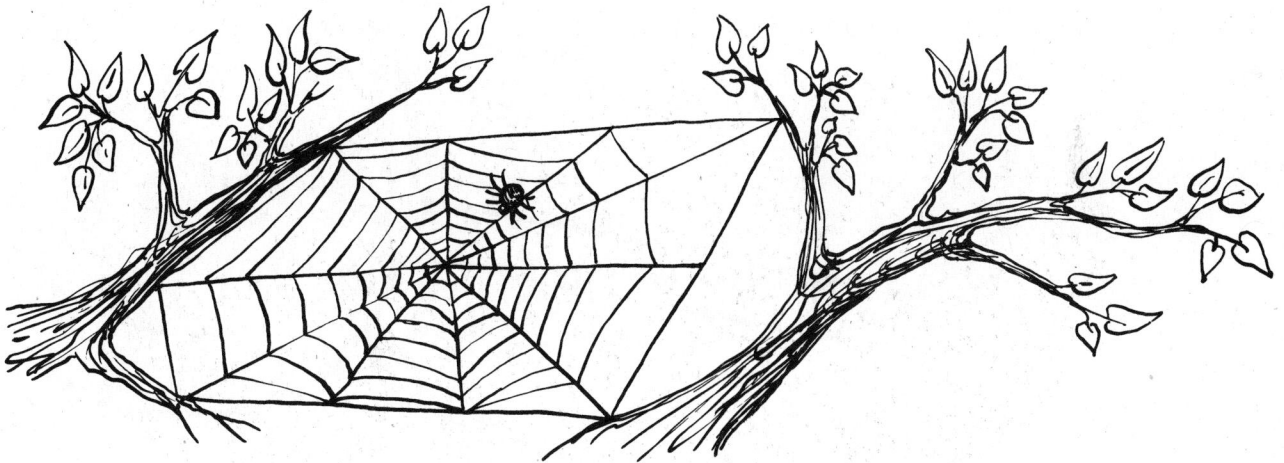

© HMH Supplemental Publishers Inc. All rights reserved.

Name _____ Date _____

Making Inferences Worksheet

Story Title _____

Complete the Following Footprints based on what you've read.

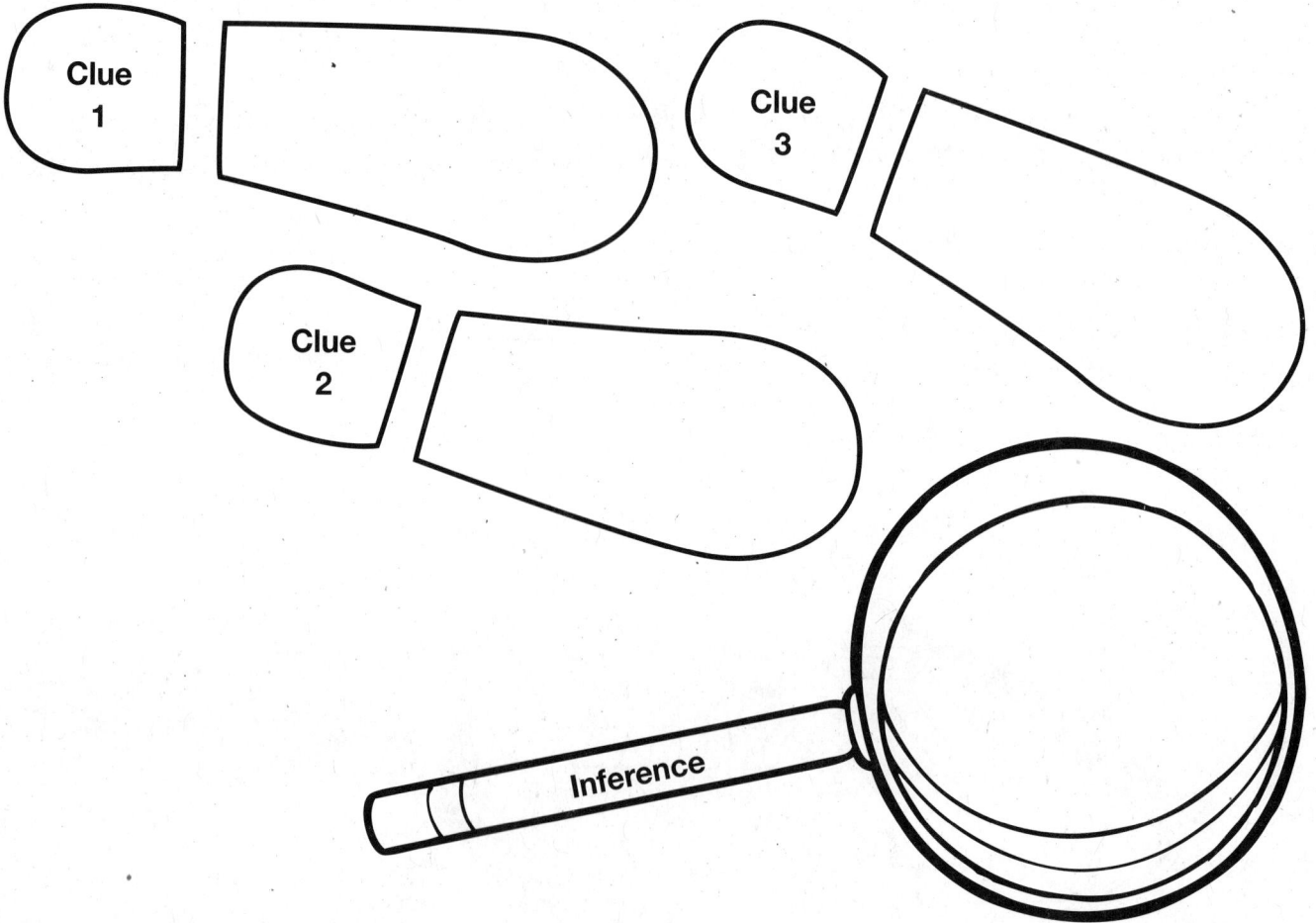

Clue 1

Clue 3

Clue 2

Inference

Summary: Use the information in the Following Footprints to write a summary of the reading.

_____

_____

_____

Forming Generalizations

Presentation and Model

Strategy: Forming sound generalizations based on what you read

When you read specific information about a topic and then come up with a broader statement about that topic, you are forming a generalization. Another way to think about generalizations is that they are general rules or ideas based on specific facts and observations.

Read the article below.

In the early days of our country, a letter was often delivered by a traveler who happened to be going in the right direction. It might change hands many times before reaching its recipient. Many letters were left at taverns or inns near the desired destination, and there they stayed until someone came to pick them up.

Letters that traveled in this manner could take months to reach the people to whom they were written. One attempt to move letters faster was the famed Pony Express. Though this mail route operated for just 18 months, in 1860 and 1861, it made history. Mail left Missouri and traveled, in the hands of many riders, 1,800 miles to California in just 10 days! The completion of telegraph lines from coast to coast could deliver a message the same day, and put the Pony Express out of business.

Complete the Generalization Pyramid based on what you've read.

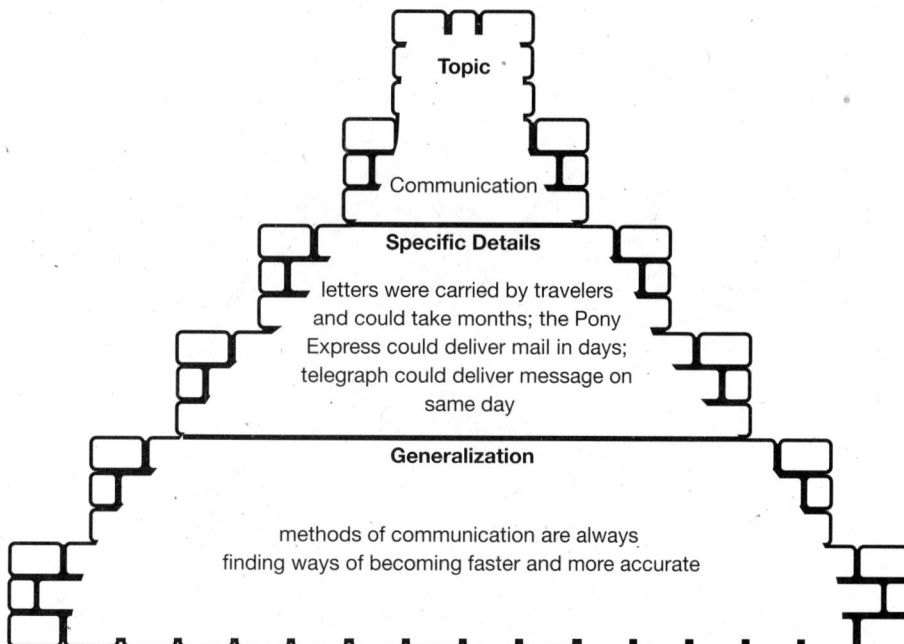

Topic

Communication

Specific Details

letters were carried by travelers and could take months; the Pony Express could deliver mail in days; telegraph could deliver message on same day

Generalization

methods of communication are always finding ways of becoming faster and more accurate

Summary: Use the information in the Generalization Pyramid to write a summary of the article.

Letters in our country's early days had to be carried by hand for many miles and might take

months to reach their destination, but telegraph lines brought faster communication.

© HMH Supplemental Publishers Inc. All rights reserved.

Forming Generalizations

Read the article below.

Hard Working Animals

For centuries, the humble donkey and the strong ox were used as pack animals. In fact, these two creatures were the first animals pressed into service to help humans move things from here to there. Donkeys and oxen carried or pulled heavy loads so that people's hands were free for other work. Around the world, people began to find uses for other animals, too. Llamas, elephants, and camels are also good workers that can carry heavy loads. Much later, horses were put to work as pack and draft animals, pulling sleds and sleighs.

Even today, with modern machinery available in many nations, all of these animals are still used for carrying heavy loads in places around the world. Of course, these animals must be fed daily and cared for. Still, they make more interesting companions than tractors!

Complete the Forming Generalizations Worksheet for this article.

© HMH Supplemental Publishers Inc. All rights reserved.

Forming Generalizations

Read the article below.

Chores Around the World

Children all around the world have chores to do. But the chores children do in one part of the world may vary greatly from those children do elsewhere.

In modern American cities, children often help out with dishes and laundry. These chores are not hard, because hot, clean water comes right out of the faucet. Many homes have automatic dishwashers that do most of the work. All the child has to do is put dirty dishes in and take clean dishes out. Laundry is automated, too. Machines do the washing, rinsing, and drying. Children only have to put the clean clothes away.

In many places, on the other hand, these chores must be done the hard way. In homes with no running water, children must either bring water from a well or other source to their homes, usually in buckets, or take anything that needs to be washed to the water. Either way, these children become accustomed, early in life, to carrying heavy loads of water. Clothes are not washed as often as they might be in city homes, and sunlight takes care of drying the wet clothes.

Complete the Forming Generalizations Worksheet for this article.

© HMH Supplemental Publishers Inc. All rights reserved.

Name _____   Date _____

Forming Generalizations Worksheet

Story Title _____

Complete the Generalization Pyramid based on what you've read.

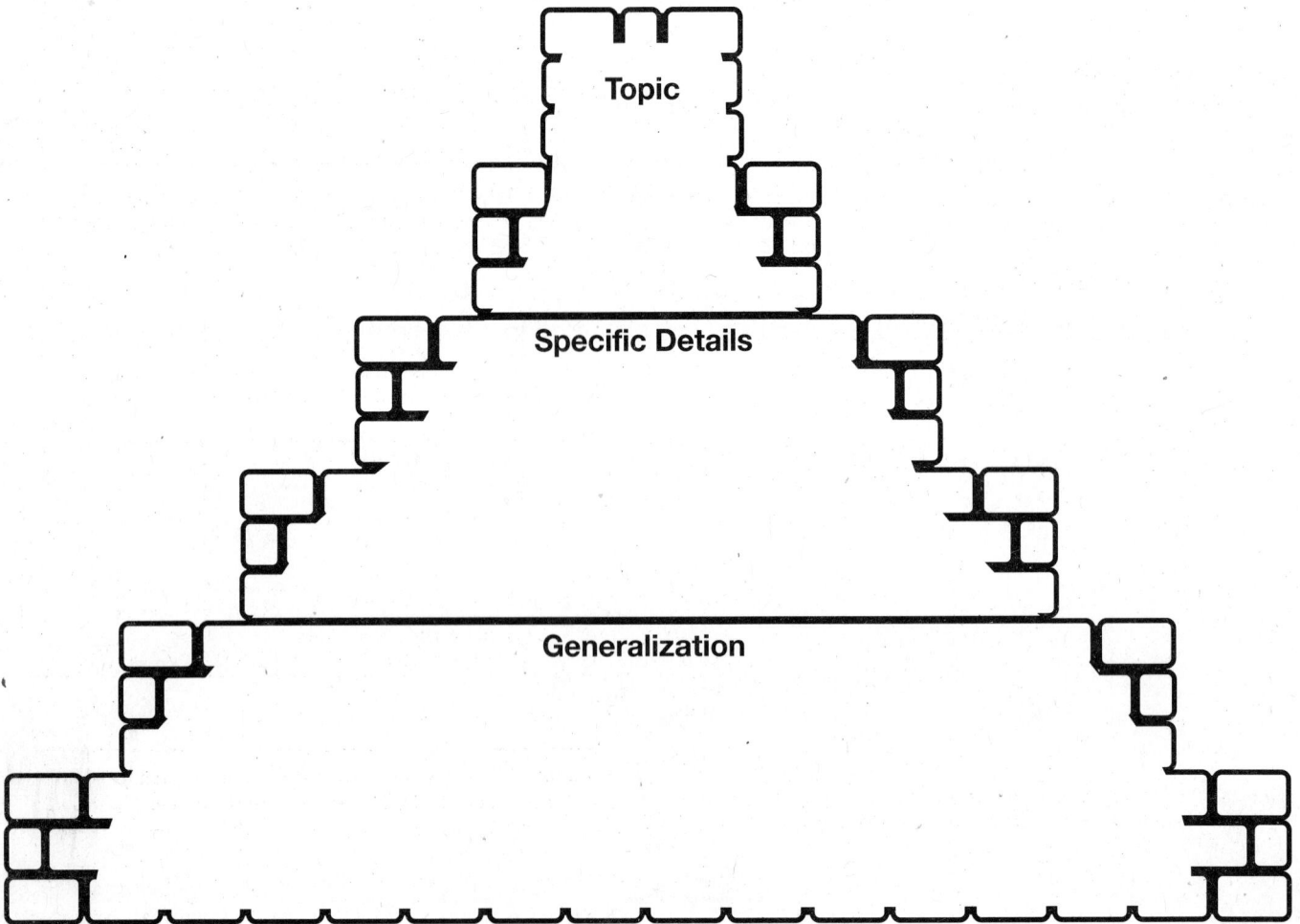

Topic

Specific Details

Generalization

Summary: Use the information in the Generalization Pyramid to write a summary of the reading.

_____

_____

_____

© HMH Supplemental Publishers Inc. All rights reserved.
Forming Generalizations
Summarizing Strategies Grade 6, SV 9781419099908

Possible Answers

Page 6
Game Night

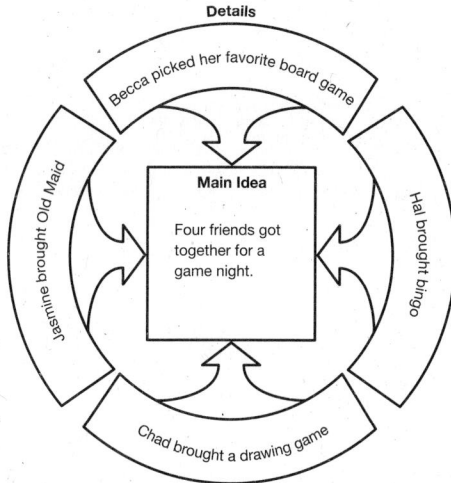

Details

Becca picked her favorite board game

Jasmine brought Old Maid

Hal brought bingo

Main Idea
Four friends got together for a game night.

Chad brought a drawing game

Summary: Four friends had a game night at Becca's house. They had refreshments and several different games.

Page 7
Amanda's Arm

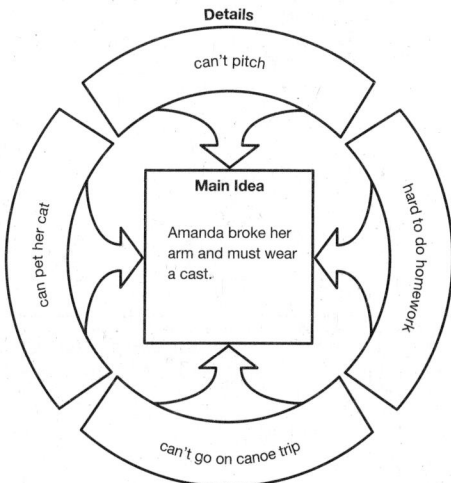

Details

can't pitch

can pet her cat

hard to do homework

Main Idea
Amanda broke her arm and must wear a cast.

can't go on canoe trip

Summary: Amanda broke her arm and had to wear a cast. There were many things she wouldn't be able to do for four weeks, but she could still pet her cat.

Page 10
A Quick Note

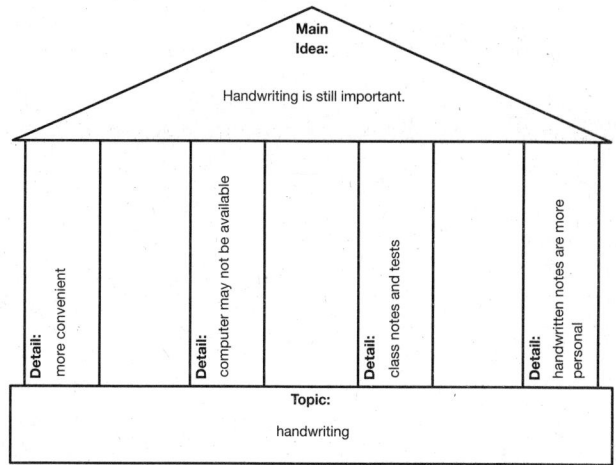

Main Idea:
Handwriting is still important.

Detail: more convenient

Detail: computer may not be available

Detail: class notes and tests

Detail: handwritten notes are more personal

Topic:
handwriting

Summary: While typing things on computers or phones has become more common, handwriting is still a very important skill.

Page 11
Poison Ivy

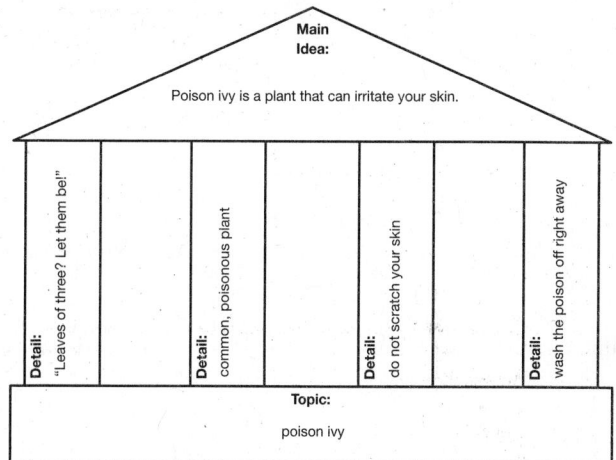

Main Idea:
Poison ivy is a plant that can irritate your skin.

Detail: "Leaves of three? Let them be!"

Detail: common, poisonous plant

Detail: do not scratch your skin

Detail: wash the poison off right away

Topic:
poison ivy

Summary: Poison ivy is a common plant that can irritate your skin. Try to avoid plants with three leaves. If you touch it, wash the area as soon as possible.

© HMH Supplemental Publishers Inc. All rights reserved.
Summarizing Strategies Grade 6, SV 9781419099908

Page 14
A Folk Music Legend

died homeless and broke

had no lessons or training

Main Idea
Foster was gifted musician but bad businessman

wrote successful songs but got no credit

"My Old Kentucky Home" and "Camptown Races"

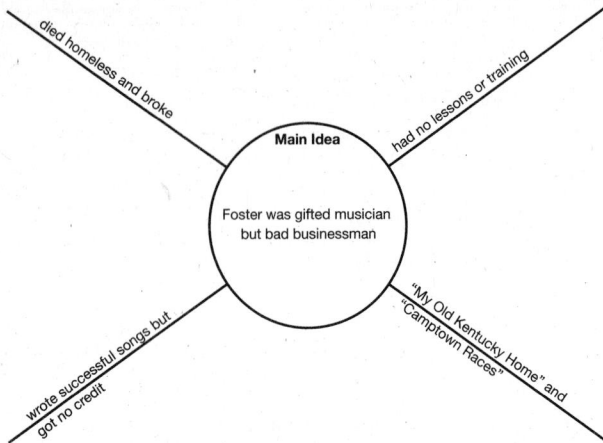

Summary: Stephen Foster was an American musician who wrote many popular songs. His musical talent did not bring him success, and he died young and poor.

Page 15
Horses, Horses, Horses!

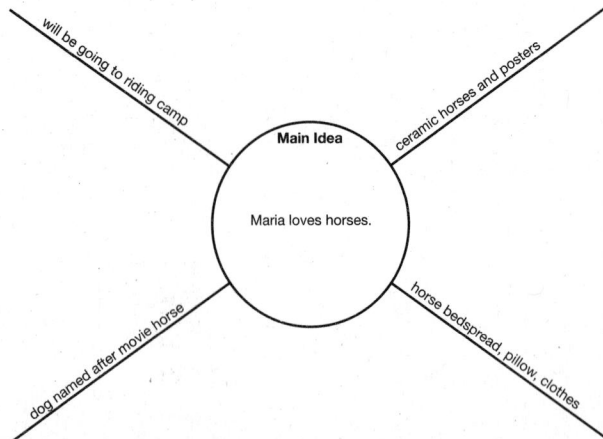

will be going to riding camp

ceramic horses and posters

Main Idea
Maria loves horses.

dog named after movie horse

horse bedspread, pillow, clothes

Summary: Maria loves horses and has many horse-themed items. She will soon have the chance to learn to ride and care for horses.

Page 18
Forgive and Forget

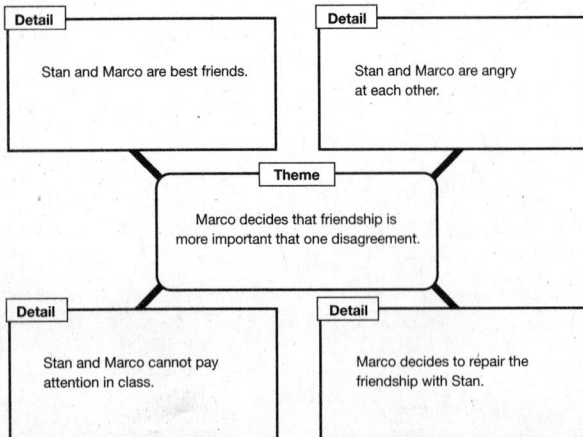

Detail	Detail
Stan and Marco are best friends.	Stan and Marco are angry at each other.

Theme
Marco decides that friendship is more important that one disagreement.

Detail	Detail
Stan and Marco cannot pay attention in class.	Marco decides to repair the friendship with Stan.

Summary: Two friends fight all day over a remark, but one friend decides to set aside his anger and make the friendship work again.

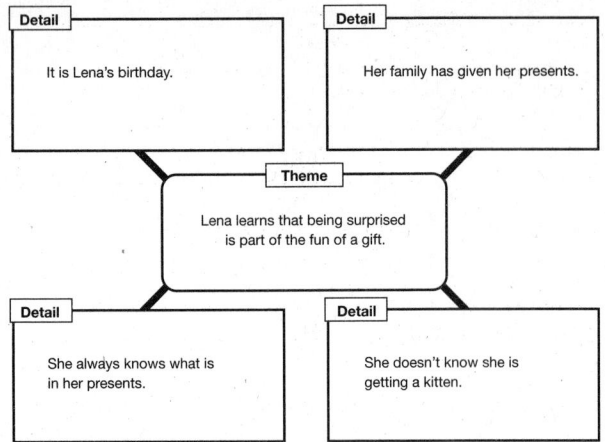

Page 19
The Big Surprise

Detail	Detail
It is Lena's birthday.	Her family has given her presents.

Theme
Lena learns that being surprised is part of the fun of a gift.

Detail	Detail
She always knows what is in her presents.	She doesn't know she is getting a kitten.

Summary: Lena always knows what is in her birthday presents, but this year, she gets a surprise. She finds that being surprised can be as fun as getting a present.

Page 22
Wasps—Busy as Bees

How Topics Are Alike		How Topics Are Different
All wasps can sting, so people should be cautious around them. Wasps help pollinate flowers and crops. Wasps eat pests that destroy crops.	**Topic 1:** paper wasp	This wasp builds its nest out of paper.
	Topic 2: yellow jacket	This wasp builds a large nest in the ground.
	Topic 3: potter wasp	This wasp builds a jug-like nest on a twig.

Summary: Wasps, though they can sting, help people and nature by pollinating and protecting crops. Different kinds of wasps build different kinds of nests.

Page 23
Roger's Collections

How Topics Are Alike		How Topics Are Different
Each collection is well cared for. Each collection has value and may become more valuable over time.	**Topic 1:** stamp collection	Stamps are old, new, from different countries. Stamps are stored in book. Roger trades stamps on line and has a lot of stamps.
	Topic 2: baseball card collection	Roger has only a few cards but wants to save up for rare cards. He has one valuable card that is framed.
	Topic 3: coin collection	Roger has many coins already. He studies their value in books.

Summary: Roger loves to collect things and hopes to build several valuable collections. He has a large stamp collection, a small baseball card collection, and a valuable coin collection.

Page 26
JoJo Has the Jitters

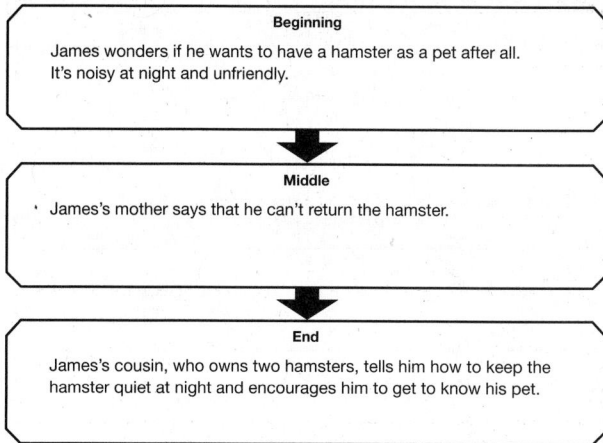

Beginning
James wonders if he wants to have a hamster as a pet after all. It's noisy at night and unfriendly.

⬇

Middle
James's mother says that he can't return the hamster.

⬇

End
James's cousin, who owns two hamsters, tells him how to keep the hamster quiet at night and encourages him to get to know his pet.

Summary: James finally gets the hamster he's wanted for a pet, but he finds that it is not an easy pet to care for. His cousin advises and encourages him.

Page 27
Ned and the Noise

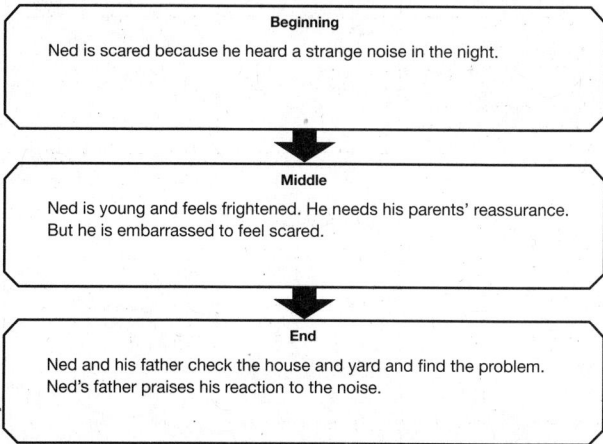

Beginning
Ned is scared because he heard a strange noise in the night.

⬇

Middle
Ned is young and feels frightened. He needs his parents' reassurance. But he is embarrassed to feel scared.

⬇

End
Ned and his father check the house and yard and find the problem. Ned's father praises his reaction to the noise.

Summary: A noise in the night scares Ned, so he wakes up his parents. Together, he and his dad find the source of the noise, and Ned's father thanks him for his help.

Page 30
New Book Order

	Humor	Biography	Mystery/ Adventure	Science/ Nature
How Many?	13	4	23	8
Most checked out?			✓	
Least checked out?		✓		

Summary: The library took a survey to see what kinds of new books to order. Almost half the books checked out were mysteries or adventures, and many humor books were checked out as well.

Page 31
Where Should We Go?

	Science Museum	Living History Farm	Wildflower Garden	Zoo
How many?	24	18	11	19
Favorite?	✓			
Least favorite?			✓	

Summary: The teachers let the students vote on where to go on the spring field trip. It was a very close race, but the students chose the science museum.

Page 34
The Clubhouse

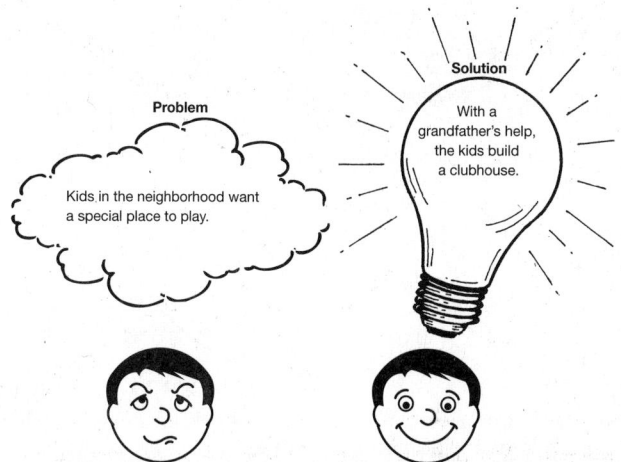

Problem: Kids in the neighborhood want a special place to play.

Solution: With a grandfather's help, the kids build a clubhouse.

Summary: Children in a neighborhood come together to build a special place to play.

Page 35
Jason's Pile of Homework

Problem: Jason feels overwhelmed by his homework.

Solution: Mom provides a good work environment and snacks.

Summary: Jason thinks that he will never finish all his homework, but his mother creates a quiet place for him to study and gets him snacks to keep him going.

Page 38
The Fox's Tale

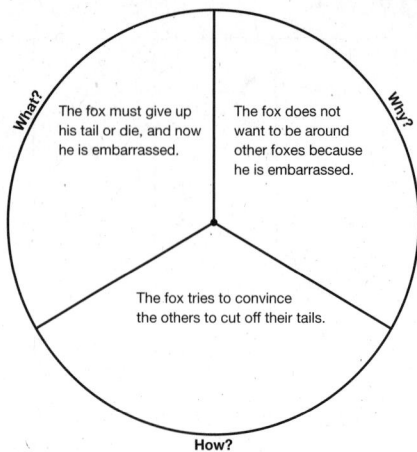

What? The fox must give up his tail or die, and now he is embarrassed.

Why? The fox does not want to be around other foxes because he is embarrassed.

How? The fox tries to convince the others to cut off their tails.

Summary: A fox loses his tail and is embarrassed. He tries to trick others into losing theirs, but a wise old fox sees through the trick.

Page 39
Lost and Found

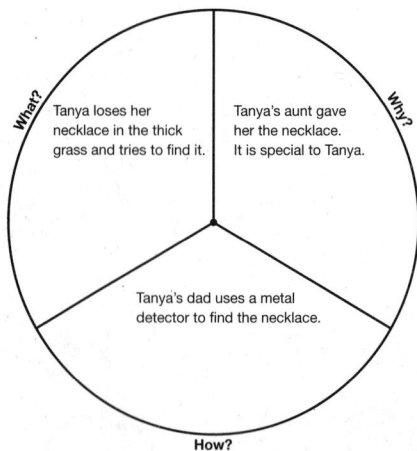

What? Tanya loses her necklace in the thick grass and tries to find it.

Why? Tanya's aunt gave her the necklace. It is special to Tanya.

How? Tanya's dad uses a metal detector to find the necklace.

Summary: Tanya learns a lesson about taking care of fragile things when she loses a special necklace while playing. Her father helps her find the necklace.

Page 42
The Best Neighbors Around

Character's name: Mrs. Johnson and her neighbors

	Action	Motivation
1.	Mrs. Johnson bakes cookies for new neighbors.	She is a caring person.
2.	Mrs. Johnson listens to children and helps people with their problems.	She likes to help others.
3.	The neighbors take cards, gifts, and flowers to Mrs. Johnson in the hospital.	They appreciate what a good and caring neighbor she is.
4.	The neighbors welcome Mrs. Johnson home and cook for her.	They want to give back for all that she has done for them.

Summary: Mrs. Johnson's caring nature causes her neighbors to appreciate and care for her. When she gets sick, they all pitch in to help out.

Page 43
Teaching Mutt

Character's name: Mutt

	Action	Motivation
1.	Mutt pesters Chas to get out of bed.	He needs to go out.
2.	Mutt pesters Chas for food.	He is hungry.
3.	Mutt pesters Chas to play and pet him.	He is bored, and pestering gets him what he wants.
4.	Mutt learns to behave better.	Mutt is taught that pestering is wrong.

Summary: Mutt is a dog that pesters to get what he wants, but a trainer helps him learn to ask politely instead.

Page 46
It's the Thought that Counts

Character's Name: Morris

What the Character Wants
to surprise his dad with a celebration dinner

What the Character Thinks
he can handle cooking dinner

How the Character Feels
happy for dad, and then overwhelmed

What the Character Says
I must be more nervous about cooking than I thought. Time for Plan B.

What the Character Does
drops salad, breaks glasses and plate, forgets cheese, orders pizza

Summary: Morris wants to cook a celebration dinner for his dad. He quickly becomes overwhelmed and ends up ordering pizza.

© HMH Supplemental Publishers Inc. All rights reserved.

Page 47
A Work of Art

Character's Name
Martin

What the Character Wants
to show everyone the model he has worked on

What the Character Thinks
A space shuttle model will remind him of his trip.

How the Character Feels
proud and excited about his model

What the Character Says
Painting them and adding decals so that they look just right is the part I love.

What the Character Does
builds model, looks at pictures, unveils model

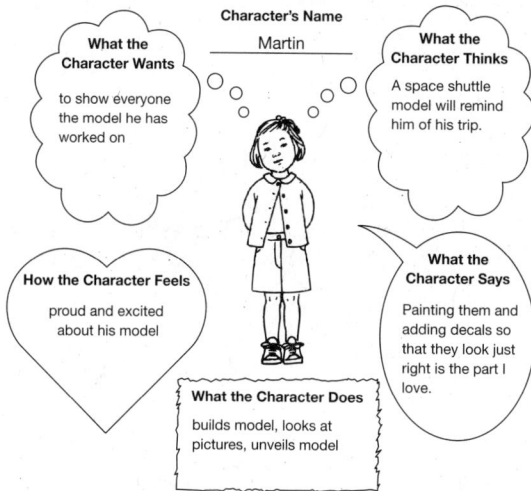

Summary: Martin builds a model as a reminder of a trip. He loves building models and making them as realistic as he can. He invites his friends to see it.

Page 50
One More Time

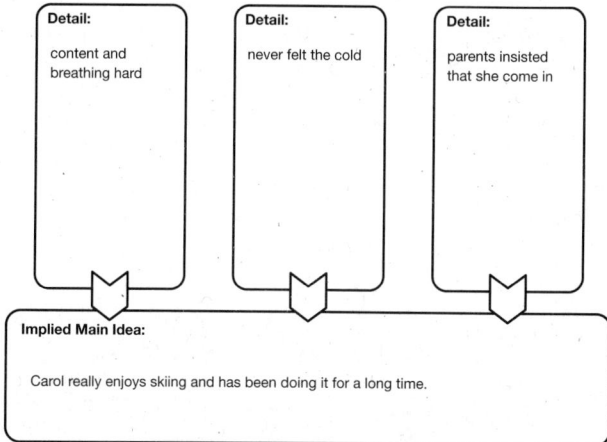

Detail:
content and breathing hard

Detail:
never felt the cold

Detail:
parents insisted that she come in

Implied Main Idea:
Carol really enjoys skiing and has been doing it for a long time.

Summary: Carol loves to ski. She is very good at it and would stay out skiing as long as she could.

Page 51
The Hippo

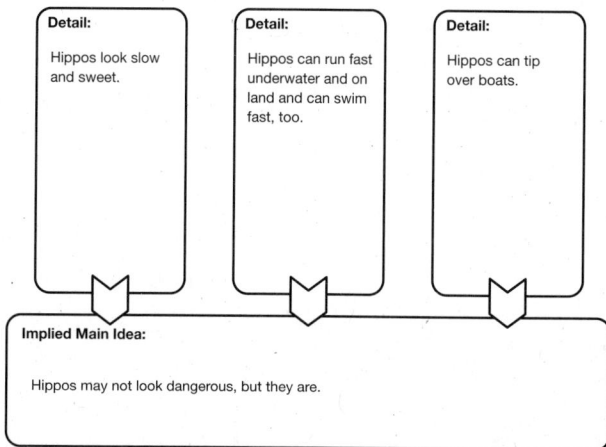

Detail:
Hippos look slow and sweet.

Detail:
Hippos can run fast underwater and on land and can swim fast, too.

Detail:
Hippos can tip over boats.

Implied Main Idea:
Hippos may not look dangerous, but they are.

Summary: Hippos in zoos may look harmless, but in the wild, these animals can endanger humans.

Page 54
How the Body Uses Fat

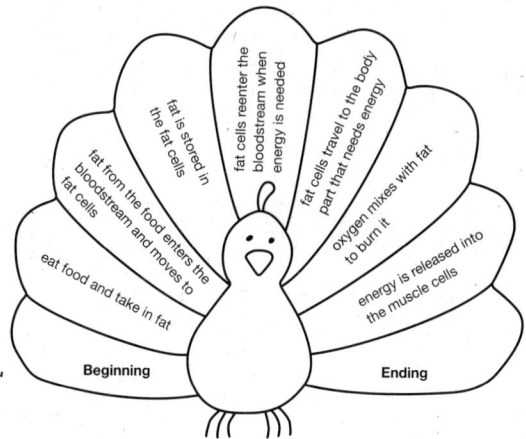

fat cells reenter the bloodstream when energy is needed

fat is stored in the fat cells

fat from the food enters the bloodstream and moves to fat cells

fat cells travel to the body part that needs energy

oxygen mixes with fat to burn it

eat food and take in fat

energy is released into the muscle cells

Beginning

Ending

Summary: Your body stores fat from the food you eat in fat cells and releases it into the bloodstream when more energy is needed.

Page 55
The New Tank

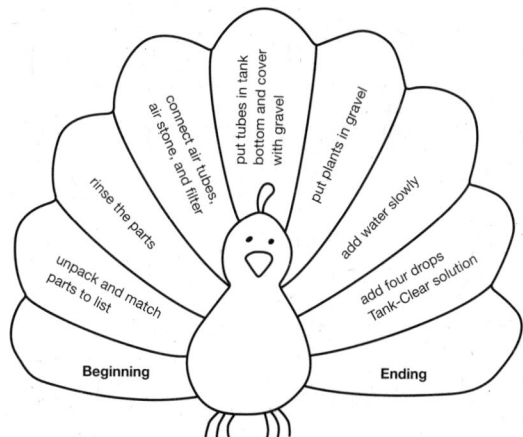

put tubes in tank bottom and cover with gravel

connect air tubes, air stone, and filter

put plants in gravel

rinse the parts

add water slowly

unpack and match parts to list

add four drops Tank-Clear solution

Beginning

Ending

Summary: Sergio explains that tank assembly requires unpacking and rinsing parts, assembling air tubes and placing them in the tank, adding gravel, and adding and treating water.

Page 58
Sheep Around the World

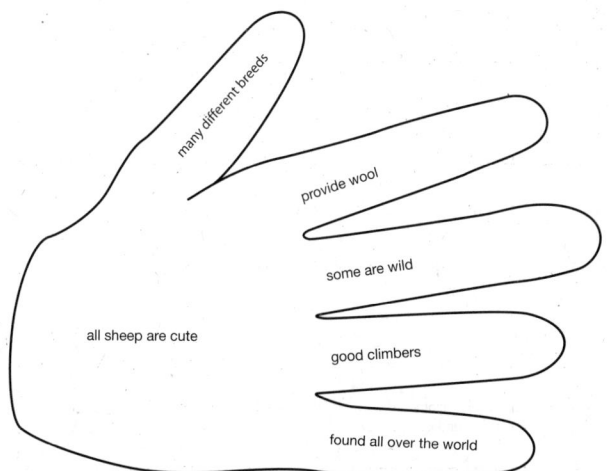

many different breeds

provide wool

some are wild

all sheep are cute

good climbers

found all over the world

Summary: Many kinds of sheep are raised across the world for food, income, and wool. Some sheep are raised by shepherds while others are wild.

Page 59
A Slithery Friend

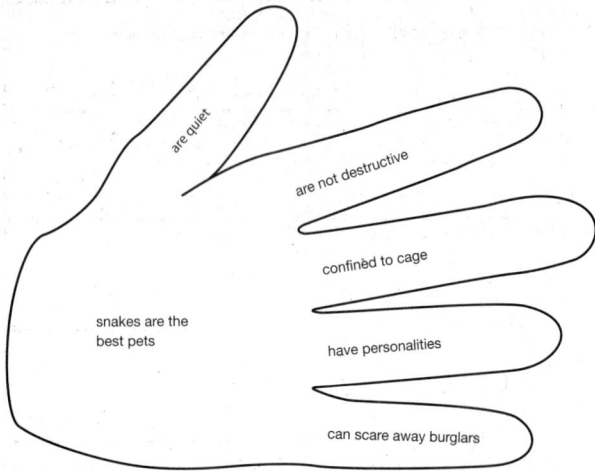

- are quiet
- are not destructive
- confined to cage
- have personalities
- snakes are the best pets
- can scare away burglars

Summary: A snake can be a good pet for people who want a quiet, peaceful pet that is easy to care for.

Page 62
Playing Solo

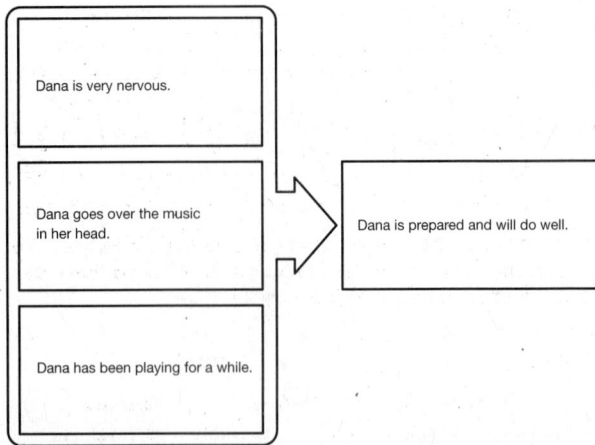

Dana is very nervous.

Dana goes over the music in her head.

Dana has been playing for a while.

→ Dana is prepared and will do well.

Summary: Dana sits nervously waiting for her turn to play for the audience and judges. She has been preparing and has been doing this for a while. She takes the stage.

Page 63
Gone Fishing

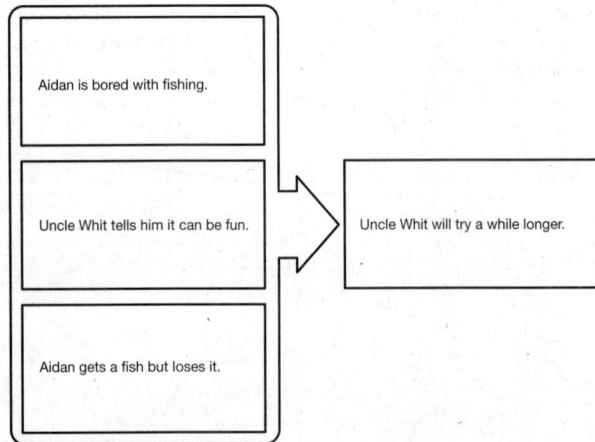

Aidan is bored with fishing.

Uncle Whit tells him it can be fun.

Aidan gets a fish but loses it.

→ Uncle Whit will try a while longer.

Summary: Aidan and Uncle Whit are fishing. Aidan is bored and wants to go, but Uncle Whit keeps telling him to wait a little longer because fishing can be fun.

Page 66
Picture Perfect

Cause
Stefan worked very hard for months on a scrapbook for a photo contest.

Effect
He won first prize.

Summary: Stefan's put a lot of effort into his scrapbook. His months of hard work resulted in his winning first prize in the photography contest.

Page 67
I See the Moon

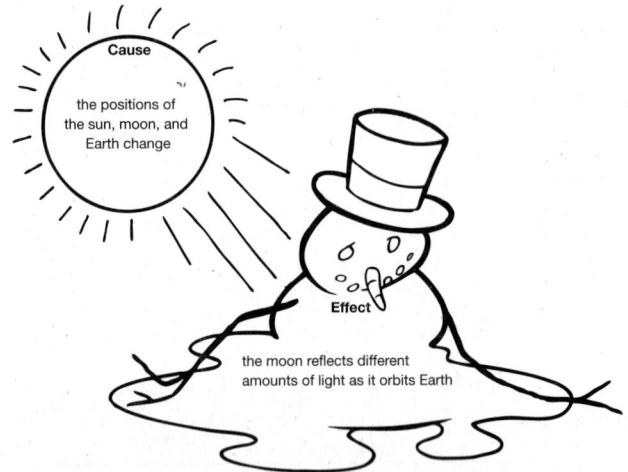

Cause
the positions of the sun, moon, and Earth change

Effect
the moon reflects different amounts of light as it orbits Earth

Summary: Because the sun, Earth, and moon change positions, the amount of sunlight reflected from the moon to Earth changes over time. This causes the phases of the moon.

© HMH Supplemental Publishers Inc. All rights reserved.

Page 70
Wayne Needs a Plan

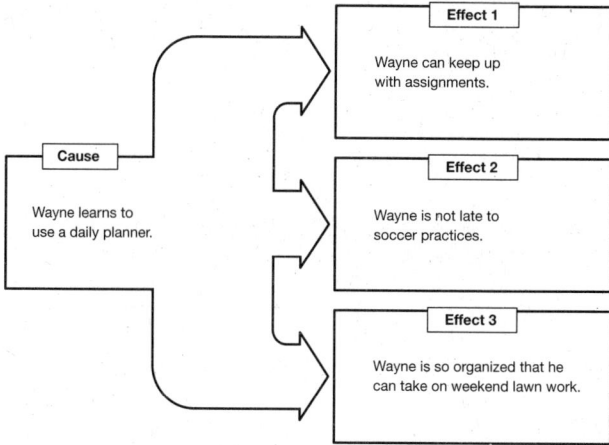

Cause		Effect 1
Wayne learns to use a daily planner.	→	Wayne can keep up with assignments.

Effect 2
Wayne is not late to soccer practices.

Effect 3
Wayne is so organized that he can take on weekend lawn work.

Summary: Because he learns to use a day planner, Wayne is able to organize and keep up with his school, sports, and work schedule.

Page 71
Trash to Treasure

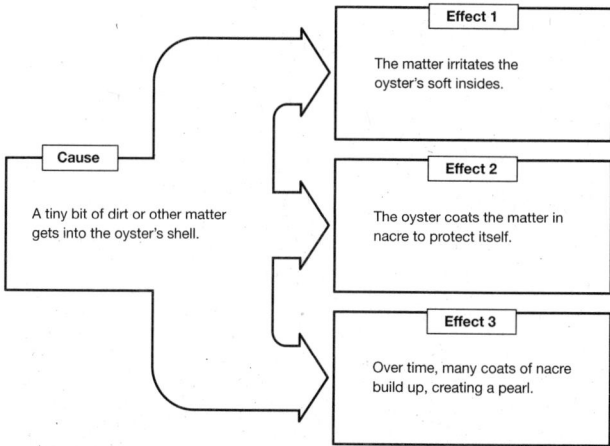

Cause
A tiny bit of dirt or other matter gets into the oyster's shell.

Effect 1
The matter irritates the oyster's soft insides.

Effect 2
The oyster coats the matter in nacre to protect itself.

Effect 3
Over time, many coats of nacre build up, creating a pearl.

Summary: Pearls form when oysters protect themselves against irritating matter that slips inside their shells.

Page 74
Calling All Neighborhood Parents!

To Inform Did I learn something as I read? ✓ Yes ___ No	To Entertain Did I smile or laugh as I read? ___ Yes ✓ No
To Persuade Me to Think Did the reading ask me to change what I think about something? ___ Yes ✓ No	To Persuade Me to Act Did the reading ask me to do something or change my behavior? ✓ Yes ___ No

What was the author's main purpose?

to persuade people to attend meeting

What was the author's secondary purpose, if any?

to inform about meeting

Summary: The author wants to persuade people to attend a meeting about creating a new park. The author also gives basic information about the meeting time and place.

Page 75
We All Need Vacations

To Inform Did I learn something as I read? ___ Yes ✓ No	To Entertain Did I smile or laugh as I read? ✓ Yes ___ No
To Persuade Me to Think Did the reading ask me to change what I think about something? ___ Yes ✓ No	To Persuade Me to Act Did the reading ask me to do something or change my behavior? ___ Yes ✓ No

What was the author's main purpose?

to entertain

What was the author's secondary purpose, if any?

to entertain

Summary: In the year 2030 robots do all the work, and people just play, read, and think. People actually pay money to take vacations where they get to do work.

Page 78
The Hard Truth

What you read	What you know	Conclusion
Mike broke the window and was honest about it.	It isn't always easy to take responsibility.	Mrs. Pollard works hard to teach Mike the value of honesty.

Summary: Mike broke a window playing baseball in the yard. He tells the truth when his mom gets home. She isn't happy about the window, but she is proud of Mike's honesty.

Page 79
A Cold Wind Blows

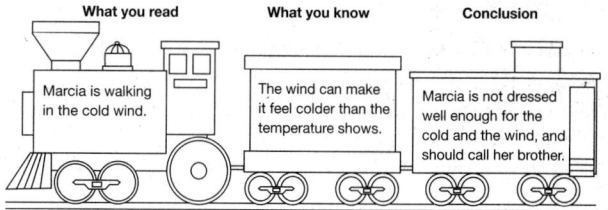

What you read	What you know	Conclusion
Marcia is walking in the cold wind.	The wind can make it feel colder than the temperature shows.	Marcia is not dressed well enough for the cold and the wind, and should call her brother.

Summary: Marcia is walking in the cold wind. Even though she is wearing winter clothes she is getting very cold. She thinks she can warm up at the library.

© HMH Supplemental Publishers Inc. All rights reserved.

Page 82
The Importance of Trees

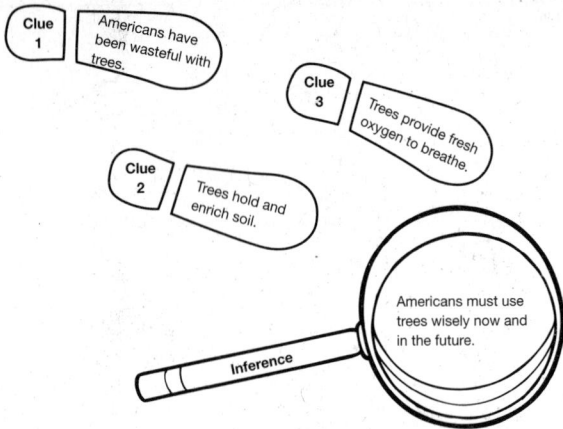

Clue 1 Americans have been wasteful with trees.

Clue 3 Trees provide fresh oxygen to breathe.

Clue 2 Trees hold and enrich soil.

Inference Americans must use trees wisely now and in the future.

Summary: Trees are often neglected as a resource. Trees serve many functions, from conserving soil and producing oxygen to providing shelter.

Page 83
Step Into My Parlor

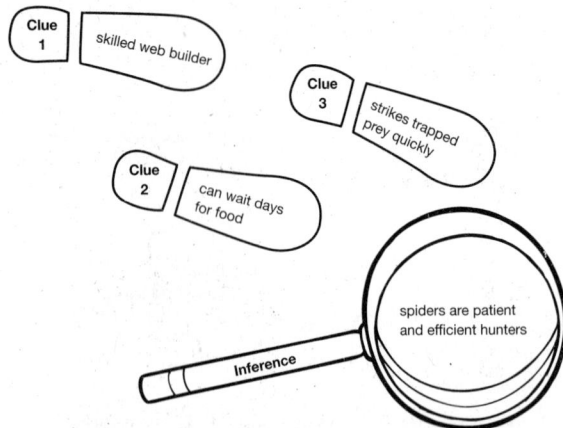

Clue 1 skilled web builder

Clue 3 strikes trapped prey quickly

Clue 2 can wait days for food

Inference spiders are patient and efficient hunters

Summary: The spider builds her web skillfully and then can wait days to catch something. She strikes her trapped prey quickly. Then she repairs the web.

Page 86
Hard Working Animals

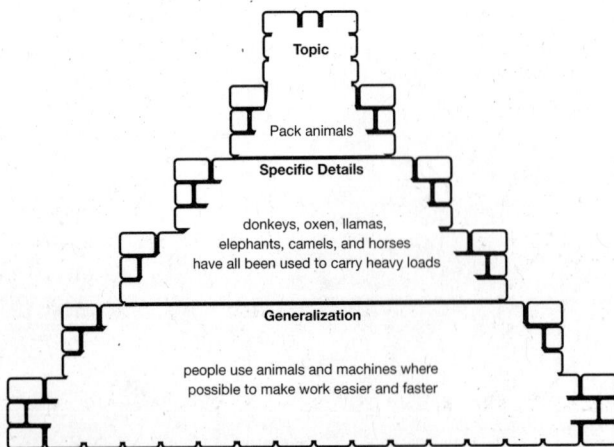

Topic
Pack animals

Specific Details
donkeys, oxen, llamas, elephants, camels, and horses have all been used to carry heavy loads

Generalization
people use animals and machines where possible to make work easier and faster

Summary: Donkeys, oxen, llamas, elephants, and other pack animals have made work easier for humans for centuries and they continue to do good work today.

Page 87
Chores Around the World

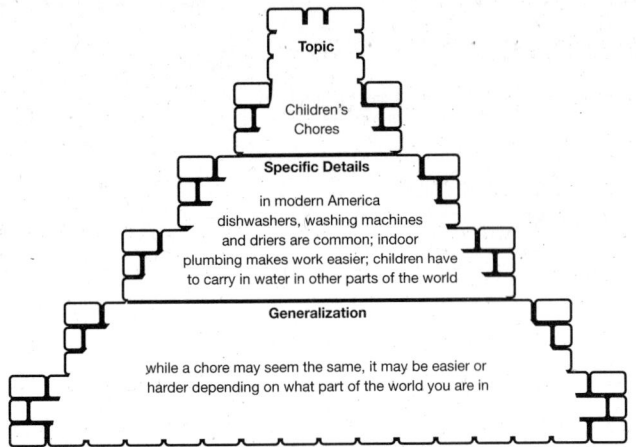

Topic
Children's Chores

Specific Details
in modern America dishwashers, washing machines and driers are common; indoor plumbing makes work easier; children have to carry in water in other parts of the world

Generalization
while a chore may seem the same, it may be easier or harder depending on what part of the world you are in

Summary: Some children do chores with the help of machines and the benefit of running water, while other children must carry water and do the hard work of cleaning themselves.

© HMH Supplemental Publishers Inc. All rights reserved.